LITERARY LANDMARKS

LITERARY LANDMARKS

*Essays on the Theory
and Practice of Literature*

FRANCIS FERGUSSON

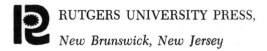 RUTGERS UNIVERSITY PRESS,
New Brunswick, New Jersey

First Printing

Library of Congress Cataloging in Publication Data

Fergusson, Francis.
  Literary landmarks.

   1. Literature—History and criticism—Collected
works. I. Title.
PN511.F4   809   75-25528
ISBN 0-8135-0815-0

Contents

Acknowledgments

I am most grateful to those who originally commissioned these essays, and gave me permission to collect them here.

F.F.

"The *Poetics* of Aristotle" was written as an introduction to *Aristotle's Poetics*, Hill and Wang: New York (1961). Reprinted by permission of the publisher.

"Poetic Intuition and Action in Maritain's *Creative Intuition in Art and Poetry*," reprinted from *Jacques Maritain, the Man and his Achievement*, edited by Joseph W. Evans; Sheed and Ward: New York (1963). By permission of the publisher.

"James's Dramatic Form" appeared in *Kenyon Review*, Vol. V, No. 4 (Autumn, 1943).

"The *Divine Comedy* as a Bridge Across Time" was originally written for a lecture for the Library of Congress, May 1, 1965.

"Molière" was written as an introduction to *Molière: Plays*, Random House, Inc.: New York (1950). Reprinted by permission of the publisher. Copyright © 1950 by Random House, Inc.

THE COLLECTED WORKS OF PAUL VALERY, ed. by Jackson Mathews, Bollingen Series XLV, "The Theater of Paul Valéry," by Francis Fergusson, in vol. 3, *Plays* (copyright © 1960 by Bollingen Foundation), reprinted by permission of Princeton University Press: pp. vii-xix.

"Oedipus, According to Freud, Sophocles, and Cocteau" was originally written for Dr. Leslie Farber for a series of lectures at the Washington School of Psychiatry.

"Ibsen's *The Lady from the Sea*" was written for the International Ibsen Seminars, University of Oslo, August, 1965.

Preface

The thought of what America,
The thought of what America,
The thought of what America would be like
If the Classics had a wide circulation . . .
  Oh well!
  It troubles my sleep.
                    —Ezra Pound (*Cantica del Sole*)

More than fifty years ago, when Pound, Eliot, and Joyce were starting out, they read the classics to nourish their own writing. They had not found what they needed in the current literature of their countries; they returned to the familiar landmarks to uncover forgotten possibilities in the ancient poetic arts. This quest seemed to them at the time to have very general value, as the quotation from Pound suggests. Joyce's Stephen Dedalus, doing his reading and elaborating his artist's creed "by the light of a few ideas from Aristotle and Aquinas," thought he was getting ready to forge "the uncreated conscience of his race," and Eliot, in his famous essay *Tradition and the Individual Talent,* proclaimed that a man should "write not merely with his own generation in his bones, but with a feeling that the whole of the literature of Europe from Homer and within it the whole of the literature of his own country has a simultaneous existence and composes a simultaneous order." Everyone knows that their generation did, in fact, produce a fundamental renewal of the arts of letters in English. And I suppose that the making of new translations from Greek, Latin, and the modern continental tongues, the reforms in the humanities curricula in the universities, and the publication of standard masterpieces in paperback must be due, at least in part, to their continuing influence.

That renewal does not look as fresh as it did years ago. Probably that is why we are now being told that the arts have died for good; that history has decreed for us only Op, Bop, anti-theater, non-music, un-poetry and the like. But the "non-arts" must succumb before long to *l'ennui, ce monstre delicat*, and then the necessity to cultivate the arts in their long tradition will be evident once more. We can't do without the arts, but they grow thin and haphazard unless the perennial meaning of the landmarks is sensed anew, in the unique situation of each generation. For that matter, there is no substitute for the pleasures of the mind and of the senses which the classics offer, even "when one merely reads to pass the time." Such, at least, is the assumption underlying this book.

LITERARY LANDMARKS

The *Poetics* of Aristotle

The *Poetics*, short as it is, is the most fundamental study we have of the art of drama. It has been used again and again, since the text was recovered in the early Renaissance, as a guide to the techniques of playmaking, and as the basis of various theories of drama. In our own time the great Marxist playwright, Bertolt Brecht, started with it in working out his own methods. He thought that all drama before him was constructed on Aristotle's principles, and that his own "epic drama" was the first strictly non-Aristotelian form.

When Aristotle wrote the *Poetics*, in the fourth century B.C., he had the Greek theater before his eyes, the first theater in our tradition. Perhaps that is why he could go straight to the basis of the dramatic art: he "got in on the ground floor." There is a majestic simplicity about the opening sentence, which we (in our more complex world) can only envy: "I propose to treat of Poetry in itself and of its various kinds, noting the essential quality of each. . . ." It still appears that, for tragedy at least, his favorite form, he did just that.

But the *Poetics* is not so simple for us as that sentence suggests. In the two thousand years of its life it has been lost, found again, and fought over by learned interpreters in every period. The modern reader, approaching it for the first time, may benefit from a little assistance.

The text itself is incomplete, repetitious in spots, and badly organized. It probably represents part of a set of lecture notes, with later interpolations. Our text is the translation of the late S. H. Butcher, who also edited the Greek from the sources.* It is one of the standard texts, probably the best now available in English. The reader will find Butcher's "Analytical Table of Contents" on pages 45-48 a useful guide on a first reading. Each chapter is summarized, and the main interpolations and omissions are indicated.

In writing the *Poetics* Aristotle apparently assumed that his readers would know his own philosophy, and also the plays and poems he discusses. Certain key terms, like "action," "pathos," "form," can only be fully understood in the light of Aristotle's other writings. Moreover, his whole method is empirical: he starts with works of art that he knew well, and tries to see in them what the poet was aiming at, and how he put his play or poem together. He does not intend the *Poetics* to be an exact science, or even a textbook with strict laws, as the Renaissance humanists tried to make out with their famous "rules" of the unities of time, place, and action. He knew that every poet has his unique vision, and must therefore use the principles of his art in his own way. The *Poetics* is much more like a cookbook than it is like a textbook in elementary engineering.

The *Poetics* should therefore be read slowly, as an "aid to reflection"; only then does Aristotle's coherent conception of the art of drama emerge. In what follows I shall offer a short reading of this kind: bringing out the main course of his thought; pausing to see what he means by his notions of human psychology and conduct; and illustrating his artistic principles by actual plays. For the sake of convenience I shall use Sophocles' *Oedipus Rex*, Aristotle's own favorite tragedy, as my main illustration. But of course the art of drama is the matter in hand,

---

* S. H. Butcher, *Aristotle's Theory of Poetry and Fine Art*, 4th ed. (London, 1932).

and the more plays one analyzes in the light of Aristotle's principles, the better one understands the scope and value of the *Poetics.*

PRELIMINARY OBSERVATIONS ON POETRY AND OTHER ARTS (CHAPTERS I-V)

The opening chapters of the *Poetics* appear to be an introduction to a longer work (which has not survived) on the major forms of Poetry known to Aristotle, including comedy, epic, and dithyrambic poetry, as well as tragedy. The *Poetics* as it has come down to us, however, is devoted mainly to tragedy, and it is in Aristotle's analysis of that form that his general theory of art is most clearly illustrated. The first five chapters should be read, therefore, as a preliminary sketch which Aristotle will fill in when he gets down to business in Chapter VI.

Poets, like painters, musicians, and dancers, Aristotle says, all "imitate action" in their various ways. By "action" he means, not physical activity, but a movement-of-spirit, and by "imitation" he means, not superficial copying, but the representation of the countless forms which the life of the human spirit may take, in the media of the arts: musical sound, paint, word, or gesture. Aristotle does not discuss this idea here, for it was a commonplace, in his time, that the arts all (in some sense) imitate action.

The arts may be distinguished in three ways: according to the *object* imitated, the *medium* employed, and the *manner.* The object is always a particular action. The writer of tragedy (as we shall see) imitates a "serious and complete action"; the writer of comedy, one performed by characters who are "worse" —by which Aristotle may mean "sillier"—than the people we know in real life. By "medium" he simply means the poet's words, or the painter's colors, or the musician's sound. By "manner" he means something like "convention." Thus the manner of the writer of epics (or novels) is to represent the action in his own words; that of the playwright to represent it by what characters, acted on a stage, do and say. One may use the notions of object, medium, and manner still, to give a rough classification of the varied forms of poetry we know in our day.

In Chapter IV Aristotle briefly raises the question of the origin and development of poetry, which includes all the forms of literature and drama. He thinks it comes from two instincts in human nature itself, that of *imitation* and that of *harmony and rhythm.* The pleasure we get from the imitations of art is quite different from direct experience; it seems to come from *recognizing* what the artist is representing; some experience or vague intuition which suddenly seems familiar. It satisfies our need to know and understand; imitation has to do with the intellectual and moral content of art, and is therefore related to philosophy. *Harmony and rhythm,* on the other hand, refers to the pleasures of form which we usually consider "purely esthetic." It is characteristic of Aristotle to recognize both the content and the form of art.

After this short but suggestive passage, Aristotle sketches the historic development of the dithyramb, comedy, epic, and tragedy, in Greece. The passage is important, for it is the starting point of modern investigations of the sources of literature and the theater in our tradition, but Aristotle has, at this point, very little to say. It has been left to modern anthropologists and historians to fill in the details as well as they could, and I shall have something to say of their theories on pages 32 to 36.

Aristotle did not have our interest in history, nor did he believe, as we often do, that the most primitive forms of human culture were the most significant. He thought that the only way to understand man, or his institutions, or his arts, was in their most fully developed, or "perfected" state. In the *Poetics* he seeks the highest forms of the art, and the masterpieces within each form, in order to see, in them, what poetry may be; and so he is led to tragedy. "Whether Tragedy has as yet perfected

its proper types or not . . . raises another question," he writes
(IV.11); but tragedy was the form known to him which best
fulfilled the aims of poetry, and most fully employed the resources of that art. He leaves room (in his usual cautious way)
for the possible appearance of other forms; meanwhile he takes
Greek tragedy, and especially Sophocles' masterpiece, *Oedipus
Rex*, as the main instance of what poetry can be.

In Chapter V Aristotle begins a discussion of comedy, but
this part is fragmentary, and not enough survives to tell us
what he thought of that art. In Chapter XXIII and XXVI he
discusses epic, but he thinks the principles of epic are only
corollaries of those of tragedy, the more complete form. It is his
analysis of tragedy, which begins in Chapter VI, that consti-
tutes the main argument in the *Poetics*.

Tragedy: An Imitation of an Action

In Chapter VI.2, Aristotle starts his analysis of the art of
tragedy with his famous definition:

> Tragedy, then, is an imitation of an action that is serious, com-
> plete, and of a certain magnitude; in language embellished with
> each kind of artistic ornament, the several kinds being found in
> separate parts of the play; in the form of action, not of narrative;
> through pity and fear effecting the proper purgation of these
> emotions.

This definition is intended to describe tragedy, and also to
distinguish it from other forms of poetry. Greek tragedy employed a verse form near to prose, like our English blank verse,
for the dialogue, and elaborate lyric forms with musical accompaniment for the choruses; that is what Aristotle means by
the different kinds of language. It is "in the form of action"—
that is, it is acted on a stage—unlike epic, which is merely told
by one voice. The "purgation of pity and fear" is Aristotle's
description of the special *kind* of pleasure we get from tragedy.

The play itself, as we read it or see it performed, is the "imitation" of an action, and in what follows Aristotle devotes his attention, not to the action, but to the making of the play which represents an action. He is concerned with the *art* of tragedy; the phases of the poet's work of playmaking. The six "parts of Tragedy" which he discusses are, in fact, part of the poet's creative labor, and should be translated, "plot-*making*," "character *delineation*," and so forth. But before one can understand Aristotle's account of the poet's *art*, one must know what the art is trying to represent: the vision, or inspiration, which moves the poet to write or sing, i.e., the "action."

The Concept of "Action"; Action and Passion

Just after the definition of tragedy (VI.5) Aristotle tells us that action springs from two "natural causes," character and thought. A man's character disposes him to act in certain ways, but he actually acts only in response to the changing circumstances of his life, and it is his thought (or perception) that shows him what to seek and what to avoid in each situation. Thought and character together *make* his actions. This may serve to indicate the basic meaning of "action," but if one is to understand how the arts imitate action, one must explore the notion a little further.

One must be clear, first of all, that *action* (*praxis*) does not mean deeds, events, or physical activity: it means, rather, the motivation from which deeds spring. Butcher puts it this way: "The *praxis* that art seeks to reproduce is mainly a psychic energy working outwards." It may be described metaphorically as the focus or movement of the psyche toward what seems good to it at the moment—a "movement-of-spirit," Dante calls it. When we try to define the actions of people we know, or of characters in plays, we usually do so in terms of motive. In the beginning of *Oedipus Rex*, for instance, Oedipus learns that the plague in Thebes is due to the anger of the gods, who are offended because the murderer of old King Laius was never found and punished. At that point Oedipus's action arises, i.e., his motive is formed: "to find the slayer." His action so defined continues, with many variations in response to changing situations, until he finds the slayer, who of course turns out to be himself. When Aristotle says "action" (*praxis*) in the *Poetics*, he usually means the whole working out of a motive to its end in success or failure.

Oedipus's action in most of the play is easy to define; his motive is a clear and rational purpose. That is the kind of action which Aristotle usually has in mind in discussing tragedy, and his word *praxis* connotes rational purpose. The common motive "to find the slayer" accounts for the main movement of *Oedipus Rex;* and most drama, which must be instantly intelligible to an audience, depends on such clearly defined motivation. But we know that human motivation is of many kinds, and in *Oedipus Rex,* or any great play, we can see that the characters are also moved by feelings they hardly understand, or respond to ideas or visions which are illusory. When one thinks of the other arts that imitate action, it is even more obvious that "rational purpose" will not cover all action: what kind of "movement-of-spirit" is represented in music, or painting, or lyric verse? "The unity of action," Coleridge wrote, in his essay on *Othello,* "is not properly a rule, but in itself the great end, not only of drama, but of the lyric, epic, even to the candle-flame of the epigram—not only of poetry, but of poesy in general, as the proper generic term inclusive of all the fine arts as its species." That is exactly Aristotle's view. He sees an action represented in every work of art, and the arts reflect not only rational purpose but movements-of-spirit of every kind.

In the *Poetics* Aristotle assumes, but does not explain, his more general concept of action. Thus when he writes (VI.9), "life consists in action, and its end is a mode of action," he is referring to the concept as explained in his writings on ethics.

The word he uses there to cover any movement-of-spirit is *energeia*. In his studies of human conduct he speaks of three different forms of *energeia*, which he calls *praxis, poiesis,* and *theoria*. In *praxis* the motive is "to do" something; we have seen that Oedipus's action, as soon as he sees that he must find the slayer, is a *praxis*. In *poiesis* the motive is "to make" something; it is the action of artists when they are focused upon the play, or the song, or the poem, which they are trying to *make*. Our word "poetry" comes from this Greek word, and the *Poetics* itself is an analysis of the poet's action in making a tragedy. In *theoria* the motive is "to grasp and understand" some truth. It may be translated as "contemplation," if one remembers that, for Aristotle, contemplation is intensely active. When he says (VI.9) that the end of life is a mode of action, he means *theoria*. He thought that "all men wish to know," and that the human spirit lives most fully and intensely in the perception of truth.

These three modes of action—doing, making, and contemplation—provide only a very rough classification of human actions, and Aristotle is well aware of that. For every action arises in a particular character, in response to the particular situation he perceives at that moment: every action has its own form or mode of being. Moreover, in Aristotle's psychology, both action and character (which he defines as *habitual action*) are formed out of ill-defined feelings and emotions, which he calls *pathos*. In any tragedy, which must represent a "complete action," the element of pathos is essential. If we are to understand the action in our example, *Oedipus Rex*, we must reflect upon the relationship between the pathos with which the play begins and ends, and the common purpose, to find the slayer, that produces the events of the story.

In Aristotle's philosophy, and in many subsequent theories of human conduct, the concepts "action" and "passion" (or *praxis* and *pathos*), are sharply contrasted. Action is active:

the psyche perceives something it wants, and "moves" toward it. Passion is passive: the psyche suffers something it cannot control or understand, and "is moved" thereby. The two concepts, abstractly considered, are opposites; but in our human experience action and passion are always combined, and that fact is recognized in Aristotle's psychology. There is no movement of the psyche which is pure passion—totally devoid of purpose and understanding—except perhaps in some pathological states where the human quality is lost. And there is no human action without its component of ill-defined feeling or emotion; only God (in some Aristotelian philosophies) may be defined as Pure Act. When Aristotle says "life consists of action," he is thinking of action, in its countless forms, continually arising out of the more formless pathos (or "affectivity," as we call it) of the human psyche. Even in pain, lust, terror, or grief, the passion, as we know it, acquires some more or less conscious motive, some recognizably human form. That is why Aristotle can speak (XVIII.2) both of "pathetic" motivation, which is closer to the passionate pole of experience, and "ethical" motivation, which is closer to reason and the consciously controlled will.

With these considerations in mind, one can see more clearly what Aristotle means by the "complete action" which a tragedy represents. In the Prologue of *Oedipus Rex*, Thebes is suffering under the plague, and the Citizens beseech King Oedipus for help: the common purpose, "to cure Thebes," arises out of the passion of fear. When Creon brings the Oracle's word, the action is more sharply defined as "to find the slayer." Each Episode is a dispute between Oedipus and one of his antagonists about the quest for the slayer, and each one ends as the disputants fail to agree, and new facts are brought to light. The Chorus is left a prey to its fear again. The Choral Odes are "pathetic" in motivation, but their pathos, or passion, is given form through the continued effort *to see* how the common purpose might still be achieved. When Oedipus at last finds himself to be the culprit, his action is shattered, and even his character as an ethically responsible man along with it. The Chorus suffers with him; but through the laments and terrible visions of the end of the play, their action moves to *its* end: they see the culprit, and thereby the salvation of the city. Moreover, they see in self-blinded Oedipus a general truth of the human condition:

> Men of Thebes: look upon Oedipus.
>
> This is the king who solved the famous riddle
> And towered up, most powerful of men.
> No mortal eyes but looked on him with envy.
> Yet in the end ruin swept over him.
>
> Let every man in mankind's frailty
> Consider his last day; and let none
> Presume on his good fortune until he find
> Life, at his death, a memory without pain.*

This marks the end of the action in more ways than one. The common purpose has reached its paradoxical success, and the Chorus (and through it, the audience) has attained that mode of action, *theoria*, contemplation of the truth, which Aristotle regarded as the ultimate goal of a truly human life.

The complete action represented in *Oedipus Rex* is (fortunately for our purposes) easy to see. But all human actions which are worked out to the end, passing through the unforeseeable contingencies of a "world we never made," follow a similar course: the conscious purpose with which they start is redefined after each unforeseen contingency is suffered; and at the end, in the light of hindsight, we see the truth of what we have been doing. Mr. Kenneth Burke has used this "tragic rhythm of action," as he calls it, Purpose, to Passion, to Per-

---

* *Sophocles' Oedipus Rex*. An English Version by Dudley Fitts and Robert Fitzgerald. New York: 1949.

ception, in his illuminating analyses of various kinds of literature. All serious works of fiction or drama represent some complete action, even so complex a form as Shakespearean tragedy. In short, Aristotle's notion is useful still; for his lore of "action" is a kind of natural history of the psyche's life.

How Plot-Making Imitates the Action

Plot-making is in bad odor with contemporary critics of poetry, because they think of it as the mechanical ingenuity of whodunits and other "plotty" entertainments. Aristotle saw the usefulness of that kind of plot-making, and offers suggestions about how to do it; but his own primary conception of plot is "organic." He sees the plot as the basic *form* of the play, and in that sense one might speak of the "plot" of a short lyric.

But he is discussing the making of the plot of tragedy, and his first definition of it (VI.6) applies only to drama: "the arrangement of the incidents." This definition is very useful, as a beginning, because it enables one to distinguish the plot both from the story the poet wishes to dramatize, and from the action he wishes to represent.

The *story* of Oedipus was known to Sophocles as a mass of legendary material covering several generations. In making his *plot*, he selected only a few incidents to present onstage, and represented the rest through the testimony of Tiresias, Jocasta, the Messenger from Corinth, and the old Shepherd. The distinction between plot and story applies to all plays, including those whose story is invented by the poet. The story of an Ibsen play, for instance, might be told as a three-decker novel, but Ibsen always "arranges the incidents" in such a way as to show only a few crucial moments directly.

The purpose of plot-making is to represent one "complete action," in the case of *Oedipus Rex* the quest for the slayer which I have described. We must suppose that Sophocles saw a quest, a seeking motive, in the sprawling incidents of the Oedipus legend. That would be his poetic vision or "inspiration," the first clue to the play-to-be. He saw this action as tragic: as eventuating in destruction, suffering, and the appearance of a new insight. At that moment plot-making begins; the incidents of the story begin to fall into a significant arrangement.

"Plot, then," says Aristotle (VI.15), "is the first principle, and, as it were, the soul of a tragedy." This is the organic metaphor which is so useful in the analysis of a work of art. By "soul" Aristotle (who was a biologist) means the formative principle in any live thing whether man, animal, or plant. Consider an egg, for instance: it is only potentially a chicken until the "soul" within it, through the successive phases of embryonic development, makes it *actually* a chicken. Similarly, the action which the poet first glimpses is only potentially a tragedy, until his plot-making forms it into an *actual* tragedy. Aristotle thought that when the incidents of the story are arranged in their tragic sequence, they already produce some of the tragic effect, even though the characters are hardly more than names. That stage would correspond to the embryo when it is first recognizable as a chicken. But the chicken is not fully actual until it has plumage and a squawk, and the tragedy is not fully actual until all the dramatis personae are characterized, and all the language is formed to express their changing actions, moment by moment. The plot, in other words, is the "first" or basic form of the play, but it is by character delineation and the arts of language that the poet gives it the final form which we read, or see and hear.

The Parts of the Plot

A complete action (as we have seen) passes through the modes of purpose and pathos to the final perception, and the plot therefore has "parts"—types of incidents in the beginning, middle, and end of the play—resulting from the various modes of action. Aristotle discusses the parts of the plot in several ways, in connection with various play-writing problems.

In Chapter XII he lists and defines the "quantitative parts" of a tragedy, by which he means the sections (rather like the movements of a symphony) in which Greek tragedies were traditionally written: Prologue, Episode, Exode, and Choric song. This chapter is probably a late interpolation, and defective; but in the light of modern studies of the relation between tragedy and the ritual forms from which it was derived, it is important. The table on page 35 shows the "quantitative parts" of *Oedipus Rex* in relation to the action, and to the supposed form of the Dionysian ritual.

Aristotle devotes most of his attention to the "organic parts" of the plot, by which he apparently means those which represent a tragic action, and best serve to produce the specifically tragic effect. They all represent the action at the moment when it is reaching its catastrophic end: Reversal of the Situation, Recognition, and Pathos, which Butcher translates "Scene of Suffering." In the best tragedies, reversal, recognition, and pathos are inherent in the basic conception of the plot, and depend upon one another, as in *Oedipus Rex*.

"Reversal of the Situation," Aristotle says (XI.1), "is a change by which the action veers round to its opposite. . . . Thus in the *Oedipus*, the Messenger comes to cheer Oedipus and free him from his alarms about his mother, but by revealing who he is, he produces the opposite effect." Notice that the objective situation does not change, for Oedipus was, in fact, Jocasta's son all along. What changes is the situation as the thought of the characters makes it out at that moment; that is why Oedipus's action changes before our eyes. The action which seemed to be about to reach a happy end is seen to be headed for catastrophe, and Oedipus's final pathos follows.

"Recognition," Aristotle writes (XI.2), ". . . is a change from ignorance to knowledge." Oedipus's change from ignorance to knowledge occurs as he cross-questions the Messenger, and then the old Shepherd. By plotting this crucial moment in this way, Sophocles has, as it were, spread out before our eyes the whole turn of Oedipus's inner being, from the triumph which seems just ahead to utter despair. The tremendous excitement of this passage is partly due to the fact that what Oedipus "recognizes" is the reversal: "The best form of recognition is coincident with a Reversal of the Situation, as in the *Oedipus*," says Aristotle (XI.2). And it is due also to the fact that this moment of enlightenment was inherent in the whole conception of the Tragic Plot: ". . . of all recognitions," says Aristotle (XVI.8), "the best is that which arises from the incidents themselves, where the startling discovery is made by natural means. Such is that in the *Oedipus* of Sophocles."

Aristotle offers the recognition scenes in *Oedipus* and in Sophocles' *Electra* (where the situation on-stage turns from despair to triumph) as models of their kind. He also briefly analyzes other more mechanical and superficial ways of plotting the passage from ignorance to knowledge. He is certainly right in calling the recognition scene an "organic part" of the tragic plot, for in good drama down to our own day such scenes are essential to the tragic effect. Consider old Lear's gradual recognition of Cordelia, as he wakes in Act V; or Mrs. Alving's recognition of her son's mortal illness at the end of *Ghosts*. The action of perceiving, passing from ignorance to knowledge, is near the heart of tragedy, and the masters of that art all know how to "arrange the incidents" in such a way as to represent it on the stage.

Pathos also is an essential element in tragedy. We have seen that the whole action of *Oedipus Rex* arises out of the passion of fear; sinks back into pathos in each of the Choral Odes, and ends in the long sequence when the Chorus finally sees the meaning of Oedipus's suffering. Aristotle has little to say about plotting the "scene of suffering," perhaps because in Greek tragedy the element of pathos is usually represented in the musically accompanied verse of the Choral Odes. His most important point is in Chapter XIV. 1: "Fear and Pity may be aroused by spectacular means; but they may also result from the inner structure of the piece. . . . He who hears the tale told will thrill with horror and melt to pity at what takes place. This is the impression we should receive from hearing the story of the *Oedipus.*" When Oedipus yells in agony, when he appears with bleeding sockets for eyes, pathos is certainly represented by "spectacular means"; but by that moment in the play we understand Oedipus's plight so deeply that the sights and sounds are only symbols of the destruction of his inner being.

In discussing the "organic parts of the Plot" Aristotle has nothing to say about the Episodes. In *Oedipus Rex* the Episodes are the fierce disputes between Oedipus and his antagonists, whereby the quest for the slayer moves to its unforeseen end; they are essential in the unfolding of the story. Perhaps the text is again defective here, or it may be that Aristotle thought the Episodes less essential to the tragic effect than reversal, recognition, and pathos. However that may be, the inner structure of the Episodes, which are public debates, struggles of mind against mind, may best be considered under the heading of Thought and Diction, and I shall have something to say of them on page 22.

Kinds of Plots

Since the vision which the poet is trying to represent in his play is a certain action, there are various kinds of plot-making appropriate to the various kinds of action. The *Oedipus* is (in Aristotle's view) the best model: the action is "complete" and the plot represents it almost perfectly. The plot is "Complex," by which Aristotle means that it includes reversal and recognition, but there are "Simple Plots" which do not include these elements. The plot of *The Death of a Salesman,* for example, is simple, for poor Willy Loman proceeds straight down to his sordid end without ever passing from ignorance to knowledge. The action of *Oedipus Rex* takes the form of "ethical" motivation as Oedipus pursues his rational and morally responsible purpose of finding the slayer, as well as "pathetic" motivation at the beginning and end of the play. But Aristotle also recognizes plays of essentially pathetic motivation, and plays of essentially ethical motivation. In our time, Chekhov's plays are pathetic in motivation, and the plot, or basic form, is more like that of a lyric than that of traditional "drama." Ibsen's plays are mainly ethical in motivation, and consist chiefly of disputes like the Episodes in *Oedipus.*

Aristotle never forgets that a play must, by definition, hold and please an audience in the theater, and his whole discussion of plot-making is interspersed with practical suggestions for the playwright. The story must seem "probable," and Aristotle has canny recipes for making it seem so. The supernatural is hard to put over, and it is wiser to keep the gods off the stage. In Chapter XVIII.1, Aristotle points out that any plot may be divided into two main parts, the Complication, which extends from the prologue to the turning point, and the Unravelling or denouement, from the turning point to the end. This way of describing the structure of a plot will sound familiar to anyone who has learned the mechanics of the "well-made play." It is a useful formula for the practical playwright, because it has to do, not with the dramatist's vision, but with the *means* of making any action clear and effective in the theater.

Aristotle's practical suggestions are still valuable, but they require no explanation, and I return to his main theory.

The Unity of the Play; Double Plots

The most fundamental question one can ask about any work of art is that of its unity: how do its parts cohere in order to make *one* beautiful object? Aristotle's answer, which he emphasizes again and again, is that a play or poem can be unified only if it represents *one action.* The poet, in building his form, conceiving his characters, writing his words, must make sure that everything embodies the one movement-of-spirit. That, as Coleridge says, is a counsel of perfection, "not properly a rule," but rather what all the arts aim at.

The plot of a play is the first form of the one action; what then are we to say of plays, like many of Shakespeare's, in which several plots, often taken from different stories, are combined?

Aristotle of course did not have Shakespeare's plays, but he did have Homer, who also combined many stories, many plot sequences, both in the *Iliad* and the *Odyssey.* And he recognized that Homer unified that more complex scheme by obeying the fundamental requirement of unity of action: (VIII.3): ". . . he made the *Odyssey,* and likewise the *Iliad,* to center round an action that in our sense of the word is one." Aristotle returns to this point in Chapter XXIII, where he takes up the epic. Lesser poets, he says, have tried to unify an epic by basing it upon one character, or one great historic event, like the Trojan War. Only Homer had the vision to discover one action in the wide and diversified material of his epics. The action of the *Iliad* (as the first lines suggest) is "to deal with the anger of Achilles." The action of the *Odyssey* is "to get home again," a nostalgic motive which we feel in Odysseus's wanderings, in Telemachus's wanderings, and in Penelope's patient struggle to save her home from the suitors. The interwoven stories, each with its plot, are analogous; and in the same way the stories which Shakespeare wove together

to make a *Lear* or a *Hamlet* are analogous: varied embodi-
ments of one action.

Aristotle did not think that tragedies plotted like the *Odyssey* with "a double thread of plot" (XIII.7) were the best
tragedies. He preferred the stricter unity of the single plot
and the single catastrophe. Perhaps if he had read *Lear* or
Hamlet he would have modified this view. Even so, his principle of the unity of action is still the best way we have to
describe the unity of a work of art, including the vast and
complex ones with two or more plots.

How Character Delineation Imitates the Action

In Aristotle's diagrammatic account of play-making, the
poet works on characterization after the action has been plotted
as a tragic sequence of incidents. Characters are of course
implicit from the first, since all actions are actions of individuals. But, as Aristotle reminds us again and again, ". . .
tragedy is an imitation, not of men, but of an action and of
life" (VI.9), and therefore "character comes in as subsidiary
to the actions." The poet sees the action of the play-to-be
first; then its tragic form (or plot), and then the characters
best fitted to carry it out with variety and depth.

One must remember that in Aristotle's psychology, character is less fundamental than action. *Character* is defined as
"habitual action," and it is formed by parents and other en-
vironmental influences out of the comparatively formless pathos
(appetites, fears, and the like) which move the very young.
As the growing person acquires habitual motives, he begins to
understand them rationally, and so becomes ethically responsible: we say that he is a good or bad *character*. When we
first meet Oedipus, he is a fully-formed character: a responsible ruler who (apparently in full awareness of what he is
doing) adopts the rational motive of finding the slayer of
Laius. But his discovery that he is himself the culprit destroys,

not only his motive, but the "character" of knowing and responsible ruler; and passion, or pathos, takes over. Old Lear, at a similar point in his story, describes the experience accurately:

> O, how this mother swells up toward my heart!
> Hysterica passion! Down, thou climbing sorrow,
> Thy element's below.

After the catastrophes both Lear and Oedipus are "pathetically" motivated, like children, and like children ask for help and guidance. In tragedy, character is often destroyed; and at that moment we can glimpse "life and action" at a deeper level.

It is easy to see how the character of Oedipus, as imagined by Sophocles, is admirably fitted to represent the main action of the play, and carry it all the way to the end. With his intelligence, his arrogant self-confidence, and his moral courage, he is the perfect protagonist. But the other characters are almost equally effective for this purpose: Tiresias, who knows the will of the gods all along, but cannot himself take the lead in cleansing the city; or Jocasta, who obscurely fears the truth, and so feels that Thebes would be better off in ignorance. The contrasting characters reveal the main action in different ways, and their disagreements make the tense disputes of all the Episodes. But all this diversity of characterization, all this conflict of thought, is "with a view" to the action of the play as a whole: that common motive which I have said is "to save Thebes from its plague, by finding the unknown culprit."

It is, of course, by the plot that this main action, or common motive, is established. It is very clear in the Prologue, when everyone wants only to save Thebes. We forget it in the excitement of the disputes, and in the fascination of the contrasted characters; but we are reminded of it again in each Choral Ode. It is the Chorus which most directly represents the action of the *play;* and the Chorus can do that just because it has less "character" than Oedipus or his antagonists. In the Chorus we can sense the action at a deeper-than-individual level, and its successive Odes, with music and dance, mark the life and movement of the *play*.

We must suppose that the actions of Tiresias, Jocasta, even Oedipus, would be quite different if we saw them apart from the basic situation of the play—the plague in Thebes. We see them only in relation to that crisis, and that is why their actions, different though their characters are, are analogous. Aristotle has a good deal to say (VI.11 and 12) about less successful kinds of character delineation. Some of our "modern poets," he says, do not make effective characters, and so their works are devoid of ethical quality. Others develop character for its own sake—for local color, perhaps, or glamour, or amusement—thereby weakening the unity of the play, which can only be achieved when the action is one. In *Oedipus Rex* this problem is beautifully solved: the characters, sharply contrasted, are full of individual life and varied "ethical quality," yet the action of the *play* underlies them all.

Aristotle offers many other ideas about character delineation, based on his observation of the theater he knew, notably in Chapters XII and XV. They are essentially practical rules of thumb, intended to assist the playwright to succeed with his audience, like his insistence on "probability" and consistency in characterization, or his notion that the tragic protagonist should usually be a ruler or leader. His observations are shrewd: but to be of assistance now they must be translated into terms of the modern theater.

How "Thought and Diction" Imitate the Action

In Chapter XIX Aristotle takes up "Thought" and "Diction" together, for they are both aspects of the language of the play. By *Diction*, he tells us, he means "the art of delivery": diction or speech as it is taught in modern schools of acting. Diction is one of the six parts of tragedy, for tragedy is by definition acted on a stage, and the actors must know how to handle its language. But Aristotle has little to say about it, because he is studying the art of the poet, who does not have to know how to speak as actors do.

Thought, however, concerns the poet directly, for thought is one of the "causes" of action. The poet works it out after the situations of the plot, and the characters, are clearly conceived. The word "thought" (dianoia) refers to a very wide range of the mind's activities, from abstract reasoning to the perception and formulation of emotion; for it is thought that defines all the objects of human motivation, whether they are dimly seen or clear and definite, illusory as dream, or objectively real. In the play, thought is represented by what the characters *say* about the course to be pursued, in each situation. That is why Aristotle identifies thought with the arts of language. "Under Thought," he says (XIX.2) "is included every effect which has to be produced by speech, the subdivisions being—proof and refutation; the excitation of the feelings, such as pity, fear, anger, and the like; the suggestion of importance or its opposite." At this point Aristotle refers us to his *Rhetoric*, where these modes of discourse are analyzed in detail.

In that work he writes (I.2), "Rhetoric may be defined as the faculty of observing in any given case the available means of persuasion. . . ." (Jowett's translation.) He is thinking primarily of a public speaker, a lawyer or statesman, whose action is "to persuade" his audience to adopt his opinion. He considers the various means the speaker may use to persuade his audience: his attitudes, his use of voice and gesture, his pauses— in short, such means as actors use. But his main attention is devoted to arts of language, from the most logical (proof and refutation) where the appeal is to reason, to more highly colored language intended to move the feelings. The *Rhetoric* is an analysis of the forms of "Thought and Diction" which the action of persuading may take.

This analysis may be applied directly to the Episodes in *Oedipus*, i.e., to the thought-and-language of Oedipus and his antagonists, in the successive situations of the plot. They meet to debate a great public question, that of the welfare of Thebes; and they try to persuade not only one another, but the listening Chorus, and beyond that the frightened city. They are thus situated as Aristotle's user of rhetoric is, and they resort to the same arts of language. They begin with a show of reason ("proof and refutation"); but as this fails to persuade, they resort to more emotional language, and when that too fails the dispute is broken off in dismay.

Sophocles' Athenian audience, which was accustomed to the arts of public speaking, would presumably have enjoyed the skill of Oedipus and his antagonists. In modern drama we find neither the sophisticated formality of Greek tragedy, nor the rhetorical virtuosity which Aristotle analyzes. But the principles, both of tragedy and of classical rhetoric, are natural, and disputants in our day—politicians or mere amateur arguers —resort to rhetorical forms, whether they have ever heard of them or not. Disputing characters in all drama—especially drama of "ethical" motivation like Ibsen's—instinctively use the stratagems of rhetoric, as they try to overcome each other with thought-and-language. The structure of great scenes of conflict, in Neoclassic French drama, in Shakespeare, in Ibsen, is in this respect similar to that of the Episodes in *Oedipus*.

At this point the logic of Aristotle's scheme seems to require an analysis of the language of the Choral Odes which follow each Episode. In glossing his definition of tragedy he explains (VI.3), "By 'language embellished' I mean language into which rhythm, 'harmony,' and song enter"—which must refer to the Odes with their musical accompaniment. And he emphasizes the importance of the Chorus in the structure of the play (XVIII.7): "The Chorus too should be regarded as one of the actors; it should be an integral part of the whole, and share

in the action, in the manner not of Euripides but of Sophocles."
We know from his remark on *Mousiké,* which includes both
music and lyric verse (in his *Politics,* VIII) that he thought
the modes of *Mousiké* imitated the modes of action with sin-
gular directness and intimacy. But he does not analyze either
music or the language of lyric poetry in any of his extant
writings. Perhaps the relevant passages are lost, for the texts
of both the *Politics* and the *Poetics* are incomplete.

One may, however, find the basis for an Aristotelian analysis of lyric language in some parts of the *Rhetoric,* and in
Chapters XXI and XXII of the *Poetics.* I am thinking especially
of his brief remarks on analogy and metaphor, which he
regards as the basis of poetic language (XXII.9): "But the
greatest thing by far is to have a command of metaphor. This
alone cannot be imparted by another; it is the mark of genius,
for to make good metaphors implies an eye for resemblances."
His analysis of kinds of metaphors is dull, and he never demon-
strates the coherent metaphors in a whole poem, as modern
critics of lyric verse do; yet the basic conception is there. His
definition of analogy is austere (XXI.6): "Analogy or propor-
tion is when the second term is to the first as the fourth to the
third. We may then use the fourth for the second, or the second
for the fourth." But this conception of analogy has also proved
fertile, far beyond what Aristotle could have foreseen. It is the
basis of the subtle medieval lore of analogy, which underlies
the poetry of Dante's *Divine Comedy.*

The Choral Odes in *Oedipus* may, like all lyrics, be analyzed in terms of metaphor and analogy. Take for example
the first Strophe of the Parode, as translated by Fitts and
Fitzgerald:

> What is the god singing in his profound
> Delphi of gold and shadow?
> What oracle for Thebes, the sunwhipped city?

Fear unjoints me, the roots of my heart tremble.

Now I remember, O Healer, your power and wonder:
Will you send doom like a sudden cloud, or weave it
Like nightfall of the past?

Ah no: be merciful, issue of holy sound:
Dearest to our expectancy: be tender!

The main metaphors here are of light and darkness: "gold and
shadow," "sun-whipped city," "sudden cloud," "nightfall of the
past." In the rest of the Ode light and darkness appear in many
other metaphors, and are associated with Apollo, the god of
light, of healing, and also of disease; it was he who spoke
through the Oracle of Delphi. The imagery of light and darkness runs through the whole play, stemming from Tiresias's
blindness, and Oedipus's blindness at the end. It is based on
the *analogy* between the eye of the body and the eye of the
mind—sight: blindness:; insight: ignorance. We may then, as
Aristotle points out, use the fourth term (ignorance) for the
second (blindness), and vice versa. Physical blindness and the
darkness of nightfall express the seeking-action of the play,
the movement-of-spirit from ignorance to insight. The Chorus
"shares in the action," as Aristotle puts it. The Chorus cannot
do anything to advance the quest, but as it suffers its passions
of fear and pity it can grope through associated images of light
and darkness, healing and disease, life and death, toward the
perception of the truth.

It is not my intention, however, to attempt a full analysis
of the poetic language of *Oedipus Rex*. I merely wish to suggest that, with the aid of the Aristotelian notions of metaphor
and analogy, one can see how the Odes also imitate the action.
The same principles apply to the poetic language of any good
play, and the best modern critics (experts in the lyric) have
made such analyses of the language of poetic drama, from
Shakespeare to Yeats to Eliot.

Song and Spectacle: Action and Acting

The three basic parts of the art of tragedy are, as we have seen, plot-making, character delineation, and thought-and-language, for by these means the poet gives the action its tragic form, and its concrete actuality. The other three parts, *speech*, in the sense of the art of delivery, *song*, and *spectacle*, all have to do with the production of the play. They are thus essential to the art of tragedy, but concern the poet less directly than the other three, and Aristotle has little to say about them. He apparently did not feel qualified to discuss music and its performance (as one gathers from his remarks on *Mousiké* in *Politics*, VIII), and he seems to have had a low opinion of theatrical production in his time. When he wrote, the great dramatists were gone; and he seems to have known a number of egoistic actors, like some of our modern stars, who made the plays into vehicles for their own personalities.

But Aristotle knew that the poet, in the very act of making his tragedy, had to be an actor. The poet does not need the techniques of voice, diction, and bodily movement, but he must, as he writes, imitate each character in his own inner being and "believe" the situations, just as a good actor does. For tragedy, as he says in his basic definition, is "in the form of actions," i.e., acted by characters. In Chapter XVII.1 and 2, he gives the poet some practical suggestions about achieving this essential quality:

> In constructing the plot and working it out with the proper diction, the poet should place the scene, as far as possible, before his eyes. . . . Again, the poet should work out his play, to the best of his power, with appropriate gestures; for those who feel emotion are most convincing through natural sympathy with the characters they represent; and one who is agitated storms, one who is angry rages, with the most life-like reality. Hence poetry implies

either a happy gift of nature, or a strain of madness. In the one case a man can take the mold of any character; in the other, he is lifted out of his proper self.

The purpose of any good technique of acting is to help the actor to perceive the action of the character he is portraying, and then re-create it in his own thought and feeling, as Aristotle says the playwright must do. The best-known acting technique of this kind is that of the Moscow Art Theater, which is widely cultivated (in several versions) in this country. The late Jacques Copeau taught such a technique, and so did the best theater schools in Germany, before Hitler. Each school tends, unfortunately, to develop its own technical vocabulary, but I think their basic assumptions may all be expressed in Aristotelian terms. They all assume that the actor's art consists in "taking the mold" of the character to be portrayed, and then responding to the situations of the play as they appear to that character. Only in that way can the actor achieve "lifelike reality." Superficial mimicry cannot produce psychological truth, fidelity to the playwright's imagined people and situations, or emotional effect on the audience. The masters of acting technique have a subtle and practical lore of action. There is no better way to understand "action," as that concept is used in Aristotle's *Poetics,* than by studying its practical utility in the art of acting.

THE END OF TRAGEDY: PLEASURE, THE UNIVERSE, AND THE PURGATION OF THE PASSIONS OF FEAR AND PITY

The question why tragedy, with its images of conflict, terror, and suffering, should give us pleasure and satisfaction has been answered in many ways. Aristotle's answers, cautious and descriptive as they are, have interested his readers more than anything else in the *Poetics,* and produced more heated controversies among his interpreters. The appeal of tragedy is in the last analysis, inexplicable, rooted as it is in our mysterious human nature, but Aristotle's observations of the effect which tragedy has upon us are as illuminating as anything we have on the subject.

He accepted, to begin with, the Greek notion that the fine arts have no end beyond themselves. The useful arts, ship-building, carpentry, and the like, provide transportation or shelter, but a play or a symphony cannot be used for anything but "pleasure." And we have seen that in his introductory remarks Aristotle suggests that the arts give pleasure because they satisfy the instincts, or needs, of "imitation" and of "harmony" and "rhythm."

When we recognize the movement-of-spirit "imitated" in a play or poem, we get the satisfaction of knowledge and understanding. The joy of Romeo when he hears Juliet's voice saying his name, the despair of Macbeth when he sees that his mad race is lost, seem to confirm something we half-knew already. The creatures of the poet's imagination do not literally represent anything in our own experience; it must be that *through* word, character, and situation we glimpse something common to men in all times and places. That is why Aristotle writes, (IX.3): "Poetry . . . is a more philosophical and a higher thing than history: for poetry tends to express the universal, history the particular."

"Harmony and rhythm" must refer, not only to music, but to the accords and correspondences that we enjoy in any beautifully formed work of art. Stephen Daedalus, in Joyce's *Portrait of the Artist as a Young Man,* explaining his own Aristotelian conception of art, offers a general definition of rhythm: "Rhythm is the first formal esthetic relation of part to part in any esthetic whole or of an esthetic whole to its part or parts or of any part to the esthetic whole of which it is a part." Young Stephen's formula is laughably pedantic, but (if one thinks it out) extremely accurate. Stephen's whole discussion shows the right way to use Aristotle's ideas: as guides in one's own thinking about art.

Why do harmony and rhythm please us? We do not know; we can only note that they do. "There seems to be in us a sort of affinity to musical modes and rhythms," says Aristotle (*Politics*, VIII), "which makes some philosophers say that the soul is a tuning, others that it possesses tuning." The notion of the human psyche as itself a harmony and rhythm reappears again and again in our tradition, notably in Shakespeare, who often uses music to suggest the health of the inner being.

Such are the pleasures we find in all the fine arts; but the special quality of our pleasure in tragedy may be more closely defined. It comes, says Aristotle, from the purgation of the passions of fear and pity. At this point Stephen's meditations may help us again: "Aristotle has not defined pity and terror. I have. . . . Pity is the feeling which arrests the mind in the presence of whatsoever is grave and constant in human sufferings and unites it with the human sufferer. Terror is the feeling which arrests the mind in the presence of whatsoever is grave and constant in human sufferings and unites it with the secret cause." Notice that these passions must be stirred by the grave and *constant*. A particular calamity with no general meaning —a street accident, for example—does not produce the tragic emotion, but only meaningless pain. Here we meet once more the universality of art: the passions of tragedy must spring from something of more than individual, more than momentary, significance. Moreover, the cause of our terror must be "secret." Tragedy, like the Dionysian ceremonies from which it was derived, touches the dark edge of human experience, celebrates a mystery of our nature and destiny.

It would seem (on thinking over the effects of a few tragedies) that pity and fear *together* are required. Pity alone is merely sentimental, like the shameless tears of soap opera.

Fear alone, such as we get from a good thriller, merely makes us shift tensely to the edge of the seat and brace ourselves for the pistol shot. But the masters of tragedy, like good cooks, mingle pity and fear in the right proportions. Having given us fear enough, they melt us with pity, purging us of our emotions, and reconciling us to our fate, because we understand it as the universal human lot.

Aristotle's word for this effect is "purgation" or "catharsis." The Greek word can mean either the cleansing of the body (a medical term) or the cleansing of the spirit (a religious term). Some interpreters are shocked by it, because they do not wish to associate poetry with laxatives and enemas; others insist that Aristotle had the religious meaning in mind. I think it is more sensible to assume that Aristotle did not mean either one *literally:* he was talking about tragedy, not medicine or religion, and his use of the term "purgation" is analogical. There are certainly bodily changes (in our chemistry, breathing, muscular tensions, and the like) as we undergo the emotions of tragedy, and they may well constitute a release *like* that of literal purgation. But tragedy speaks essentially to the mind and the spirit, and its effect is *like* that which believers get from religious ceremonies intended to cleanse the spirit. Aristotle noticed (*Politics,* VIII) that, in religious rituals he knew, the passions were stirred, released, and at last appeased; and he must have been thinking partly of that when he used the term "purgation" to describe the effect of tragedy.

In the *Poetics* Aristotle does not try to show how the various effects which the art of tragedy aims at, as its "end," are united in an actual play. The pleasures of imitation, harmony, and rhythm; the universal quality of art, and the release and cleansing of the passions, are things he observed, and mentioned in different contexts. But we may, if we like, confirm them in any good tragedy. The effect of *Oedipus Rex,* for example, depends upon its subtle and manifold "rhythm" as

Joyce defines the word; upon the pity and fear which are stirred in us, and upon our recognition, at the end, of something both mysterious and universal in Oedipus's fate. Aristotle had a consistent and far-reaching conception of the art of tragedy, and of its end; but his conception only emerges gradually as one thinks over his observations in the light of one's own experience of drama.

THE POETICS AND THE RITUAL FORMS OF GREEK TRAGEDY

For the last hundred years or more, Greek tragedy has been understood as an outgrowth of rites celebrated annually at the Festival of Dionysus. Those rites have been investigated both in their relation to the god Dionysus and in their relation to the primitive religion of the Greeks. The result is a conception of Greek tragedy which is very different from that which prevailed from the Renaissance into the eighteenth century. The Renaissance humanists and their successors saw it in "civilized" and rational terms; in our time we see that much of its form and meaning is due to its primitive source, and to the religious Festival of which it was a part.

This new conception of Greek tragedy has had a very wide effect upon our understanding of the sources of poetry in our tradition, and also upon modern poetry itself, including the theater and music. One thinks of Wagner, and of Nietzsche, who when he wrote *The Birth of Tragedy from the Spirit of Music* was the prophet of Wagner; of Stravinsky, of T. S. Eliot; of French writers as different as Cocteau and Valéry.

In writing the *Poetics* Aristotle was interested in the fully developed tragic form, and not in its ritual sources. He recognized them, however, in his account (IV.12) of the growth of tragedy from the dithyramb. The "quantitative parts" of the tragic plot which he describes are apparently traditional, and derived from the parts of the old rituals. And the "end" of tragedy as he describes it, the purgation of passion, and the embodiment of a universal truth, are analogous to the purposes of religious ritual. The rituals of the Festival of Dionysus are supposed to have included initiation ceremonies, intended to purify the neophyte by the enactment of symbolic ordeals and sacrifices; and also "rites of spring," symbolic enactments of the death and rebirth of a "season-spirit" (as Harrison calls him), upon whom the annual renewal of vegetable life was thought to depend. If these modern theories of the ritual sources of tragedy do not explain the *Poetics* directly, they may throw light upon it indirectly, by deepening our understanding of the art form which Aristotle was analyzing.

Unfortunately little is known directly about the rites of the Dionysian Festival, or about the poets, Aeschylus's predecessors, who gradually made the tragic form out of ritual. The scholars who devote their lives to such matters do not agree upon the evidence to be accepted, nor upon the interpretation of the evidence. But some of their theories are extremely suggestive, especially those of the Cambridge school, Frazer (of *The Golden Bough*), Cornford, Harrison, Murray, and their colleagues and followers. It is this school which has had the deepest influence upon modern poetry and upon the whole climate of ideas in which we now read Greek tragedy and the *Poetics*.

Jane Ellen Harrison's *Themis, A Study of the Social Origins of Greek Religion,* is a basic work of this school. It contains a note by Gilbert Murray on "The Ritual Forms Preserved in Greek Tragedy." Murray writes (page 341):

> The following note presupposes certain general views about the origin and essential nature of Greek Tragedy. It assumes that Tragedy is in origin a Ritual Dance. . . . Further, it assumes, in accord with the overwhelming weight of ancient tradition, that the dance in question is originally or centrally that of Dionysus; and it regards Dionysus, in this connection, as the spirit of the Dithyramb or Spring Drômenon . . . an "Eniautos-Daimon"

[Season-Spirit] who represents the cyclical death and rebirth of the world, including the rebirth of the tribe by the return of the heroes or dead ancestors.

Murray is referring to such mythic figures as Attis, Adonis, and Osiris, whose cults and legends are described by Frazer in *The Golden Bough*—representatives of the Season-Spirit. Murray continues:

If we examine the kind of myth which seems to underlie the various "Eniautos" celebrations we shall find:

1. An *Agon* or Contest, the Year against its enemy, Light against Darkness, Summer against Winter.

2. A *Pathos* of the Year-Daimon, generally a ritual or sacrificial death, in which Adonis or Attis is slain by the tabu animal, the Pharmakos stoned, Osiris, Dionysus, Pentheus, Orpheus, Hippolytus torn to pieces (sparagmos).

3. A *Messenger*. For this Pathos seems seldom or never to be actually performed under the eye of the audience. . . . It is announced by the messenger.

4. A *Threnos* or Lamentation. Specially characteristic, however, is a clash of contrary emotions, the death of the old being also the triumph of the new. . . .

5 and 6. An *Anagnorisis*—discovery or recognition—of the slain and mutilated Daimon, followed by his Resurrection or Apotheosis or, in some sense, his "Epiphany in glory." . . . It naturally goes with a *Peripeteia* or extreme change of feeling from grief to joy.

Murray does not maintain that the ancient rituals were all exactly the same, nor that the Greek tragedies we have exactly follow any ritual pattern. He lists all of the extant tragedies, and briefly indicates the ritual forms which he finds, in a different way, in each one.

The theory here expounded by Murray has been much criticized by other experts, and the whole field is full of disputes

Oedipus Rex (sequence of scenes)	Action of Play	"Quantitative Parts" Poetics XII	"Organic Parts" Poetics X, XI	Parts of the Dionysian Ritual (after Murray)
Citizens ask Oedipus for help, Creon brings word from the Oracle	To discover how to cure Thebes of plague	Prologue		(a Messenger often gives a Prologue—cf. Creon in the play)
chorus		Parode		
Oedipus and Tiresias	To find the slayer of Laius (rational purpose)	Episodes and Choric Song		Agon or Contest, season-spirit against its antagonists
chorus				
Oedipus and Creon				
Oedipus, Creon, Jocasta				
chorus with Oedipus		commos		
Oedipus and Jocasta		Episode and Choric Song	Reversal and Recognition	
chorus				
Jocasta, Messenger, Oedipus				Anagnorisis or Recognition and Threnos or Lamentation
Chorus with Oedipus		commos		
Oedipus and Shepherd		Episodes and Choric Songs		
chorus				
Attendant, Chorus, Oedipus Blind, Creon	To accept the truth (Pathos—Perception)	Exode	Pathos or "Scene of Suffering"	Epiphany — Pathos, with Messenger (in the play, above, the Attendant who tells of Jocasta's death and Oedipus's blinding)
Chorus alone (final lines)				

Table of the Relation between the Scenes of *Oedipus Rex*, the Action of the Play, the "Parts" of the Play according to Aristotle, and the Parts of the Ritual according to Murray.

so erudite that the non-specialist can only look on in respectful silence. But the general notion—that the ritual enactment of struggle, suffering, sacrifice, and the appearance of new light and new life, is at the root of the tragic form—is an insight of the first importance. In primitive societies the ritual is intended to assure the rebirth of vegetation, upon which the physical life of the tribe depends, after the annual death of winter. In civilized societies it comes to signify the rebirth of the human spirit through suffering, as in the Christian liturgy. In *Oedipus Rex* many very primitive elements are present: the wasting of the physical life of Thebes under its "plague," Oedipus's limp, and his mutilated eyes, signs characteristic of the scapegoat, king, or semidivine hero, who undergoes ritual combat and suffering to restore the life of the community. But in Sophocles' play these ancient savage elements represent the renewal, or cleansing, of the life of the spirit through suffering and the perception of truth.

The table on page 35 is intended to show parallels between the form of *Oedipus Rex,* as Aristotle analyzes the tragic form, and the ritual forms as reconstructed by Murray and his school. It is offered, not as a provable or disprovable hypothesis, but as an "aid to reflection" upon the form and meaning of tragedy.

Maritain's *Creative Intuition*

Creative Intuition in Art and Poetry is the most comprehensive study of those problems of the nature and meaning of poetry which concerned Jacques Maritain for many years. The title refers to the distinction between poetry itself and the arts —verse, painting, sculpture—whereby the poet seeks to embody the poetic experience he feels within himself. "There is no poetic experience without a secret germ, tiny as it may be, of a poem" he writes (p. 239). "But there is no genuine poem which is not a fruit growing with inner necessity out of poetic experience." Art and poetry are thus indissolubly connected; yet the distinction between them is of crucial importance for our understanding of the artist's psychology, and of the meaning and value of his work.

Inspiration, or "poetic experience" as Maritain prefers to call it, has been discussed since Plato. But Maritain shows that the full awareness of poetry in this sense, poetry as independent not only of Faith, morals and philosophy, but even of the forms and esthetic criteria of all actual arts and schools of art, is a modern achievement. "As to the *prise de conscience* of *poetry as poetry*," he says (p. 256) "it was only in the course of the nineteenth century that the phenomenon came about. Then, for some decades, one was able to contemplate a series of discoveries, failures, catastrophes, and revelations which were

37

extraordinarily illuminating. I believe that what occurred after Baudelaire with respect to poetry had in the domain of art as much historic significance as, in the domain of science, the greatest crises of renewal and revolution in physics and astronomy."

Maritain is uniquely qualified to explore and assess the revolution which we call modern poetry. He lived the life of art in the time and place, Paris in the twenties, when an unparalleled galaxy of poets, painters, and musicians was exploiting the "new self-awareness of poetry" in countless ways. Maritain knew intimately not only the art but many of the artists themselves, and what he says of poetry comes out of that rich and diverse life which he shared. But he shared it as philosopher, and in that respect also he is unique: who else has been able to use Thomistic insights and principles as he does, as a means of understanding the unprecedented modern world? It is his philosophy which enables him to place modern poetry in the context of a much older, wider, and more central tradition. He completes the labors of the poets themselves, bringing their new self-conscious freedom into historic perspective, and into the light of knowledge as metaphysicians understand knowledge.

The purpose of the book, which its title describes, requires that any and all kinds of visual and verbal arts be taken into account. Maritain never forgets the vast accumulation available to the modern world, what Malraux called "the museum without walls": oriental arts, primitive arts from every corner of the world, as well as the harvest of our own long tradition. He keeps the reader reminded of all this by presenting, with each chapter, a selection of plates, and a collection of relevant "Texts without Comment": short poems, bits of philosophy and criticism, and gnomic utterances by poets themselves upon their mystery.

It should be clear from this brief description that *Creative Intuition* is not to be summarized or commented upon in a short essay. Its scope is too great; and moreover much of its value lies in its form and in the exact formulations reached from time to time. Maritain proceeds by his characteristic method of delicate dialectic, *distinguer pour unir,* as he calls it. His purpose is not to present an abstract thesis, but to lead the reader to new and more exact perceptions. And the best way to read his book is, therefore, as an "aid to reflection." A consistent vision of poem-making underlies the whole, but the best way to approach this vision is by way of some problem— whether of psychology or epistemology; *Geistesgeschichte,* or taste, or criticism—which the reader himself is struggling with. The book, if carefully questioned, will help the reader to think out his own problem, and so reveal one aspect at least of Poetry as Maritain understands it.

In what follows I propose to illustrate this process by asking the book a question which seems significant to me: What is the relation between modern poetry's new self-awareness and that conception of poetry as the "imitation of an action" which may be found in Aristotle's *Poetics,* and in another form in the *Divine Comedy?*

Maritain deals explicitly with this matter in his last chapter, "The Three Epiphanies of Creative Intuition." He is considering a question raised by Waldo Frank and Allen Tate: why Hart Crane, a lyric poet of great gifts, was unable to succeed with the longer, epic form he attempted in *The Bridge.* A few modern novelists have made long and elaborate prose compositions of some poetic validity, and poets of the past have succeeded with epic or drama. But contemporary poets formed in the modern lyric tradition, and enlightened by its strict self-awareness, though they often aspire to the larger forms, seldom master them. Why? Has poetry been revealed, once and for all, as essentially brief, as Poe taught? Is Benedetto Croce right when he says that in the light of modern taste *The Divine Comedy* is not truly poetic as a whole, but only in bits?

It is in order to throw light on such questions as these that Maritain introduces the concept of "action." Frank and Tate had suggested that Crane lacked an adequate "theme" to unify *The Bridge*. Maritain proposes to substitute "action" for "theme" as the clue to the unity of the larger poetic forms. He explains that the theme—the "moral of the tale"—does not precisely relate to what the poem *is*, but rather to what the poem intends or proposes, what the poem *wills*" (p. 356). Action, on the other hand, does designate the being of the poem, its inner life, or "movement of spirit," in Dante's phrase. One may often abstract various themes from a good poem. And there are plenty of clumsy moralizing poems in which the ostensible theme is belied by the actual life we feel in them.

It was of course Aristotle who first described the arts as imitations, in their various media, of action. The key word here is the technical term *action*. Aristotle's doctrine makes little sense unless one sees that by "action" he does not mean the incidents of the plot, but an inner deed, a "movement" not of the body but of the psyche. Our words *purpose, intention,* and *motive* refer to modes of action, as that word is used in the *Poetics*. "Motive" is perhaps the best, for it is the most general, including willed and rationalized purposes at one extreme (Aristotle's "ethical motivation") and unwilled movements of spirit at the other (Aristotle's "pathetic motivation"). Action is an analogical concept, and real actions, as we observe them, are each unique. The actions of poems and plays are unique too. And only when one recognizes the particular movement-of-spirit which the poet has felt, can one fully understand the art whereby he has sought to imitate it: plotting, or the arrangement of incidents which spring from the underlying motive; character, which is "habitual action"; and the complex arts of words which also reflect the motives of the speaker. A long play or poem—even the *Odyssey*—has one action, which is, however, developed in many analogous incidents and characters.

Dante too (in *The Divine Comedy*) thought of action as the basis or "inspiration" of the poet; and of his art as imitating action as closely as possible. But he had never read the *Poetics*, and his Aristotelian philosophy came to him by way of the Fathers and Doctors of the Church. He describes action in terms of love (*Purgatory*, 18, Temple Classics edition):

> The enamoured mind falls to desire, which is a spiritual movement, and never rests until the object of its love makes it rejoice.

> Now may be apparent to thee, how deeply the truth is hidden from the folk who aver that every act of love is in itself a laudable thing.

> Because its material [i.e., love] may seem always to be good but not every imprint [i.e., the object that forms or actualizes love at the moment of attachment] is good, albeit the wax be good.

His work as poet of the *dolce stil nuovo* consists, not in following certain rules of *art*, but in imitating exactly the "spiritual movements" he perceives in his own inner being: (*Purgatory*, 24, my translation):

> I am one who, when love breathes in me, take note, and in that mode which he dictates within, go signifying.

This is Maritain's distinction between poetic experience and art. We know with what appalling candor Dante noted love's mode in his own inner being, from the deluded motives of Hell, through the changing and suffering motivations of Purgatory, to the triumphant end in the *Paradiso*, when (Canto 1, Temple Classics)

> as it draweth nigh to its desire, our intellect sinketh so deep, that memory cannot go back upon the track.

And at every point he imitated or "signified" love's modes in the modes of discourse—logical or rhetorical, poetic or dramatic —which best embodied that focus of desire and perception.

I have said that "motive" best suggests what Aristotle means by the "action" of poem or drama; and that is what Maritain means when he proposes to substitute "action" for "theme". But Maritain then reminds us that in Aristotelian philosophies of being and essence, matter and form, the potential and the actual, the concept of action has also much wider meanings (p. 358):

> Philosophers distinguish between two kinds of action—"transitive action," through which one thing modifies another, and "immanent action," which belongs to the category of quality, and through which a living agent perfects its own being. Immanent action, which tends essentially to complete in actuation the agent itself, produces at the same time a certain effect or a certain fruit (the concept, for instance, in the intellect) which remains within the agent.
>
> Assuming the Aristotelian notions of *act* as fulness or completion in being, and of *existence* as *actus primus*, primary act, and act of all acts, Thomist philosophy states that action or operation, either transitive or immanent, is *actus secundus*, an emergent terminative act, of a superabundance of existence, through which being asserts itself beyond substantial existence. For things are and exist before acting. Everywhere except in God, action is distinct from the essence of the agent and from its act of existing.

These notions show how Dante related the countless motives of his poem to a cosmological and theological framework. From another point of view, they enable us to see more clearly how the poet's creative activity completes or actualizes his own being. And, by analogy, one can see action as the *being* of the poem—to be further actualized, through the actions of the artist, in plot, then character, then language.

Maritain sometimes describes poetic intuition in terms of action, as, for example, on page 242:

In the first phase, then, in the phase of systole and unifying repose, all the forces of the soul, gathered together in quietude, were in a state of virtuality and dormant energy. And poetic intuition, still preconscious, was the only act formed within the preconscious life of the intellect, and was the secret reason for this silent concentration. It is not surprising that at a given moment this same poetic intuition, acting no longer in the manner of an hypnotic but rather of a catalytic agent, should make the virtual energies concentrated around it pass also to the act. Then, from the single actuation of all the forces of the soul withdrawn into their root vitality, a single transient motion will result, which manifests itself either negatively, by a breaking of barriers, or positively, by the entrance of poetic intuition into the field of consciousness.

One is reminded of Beatrice's explanation of the analogous (not, of course, identical) experience of beatitude (*Paradiso*, 28, Temple Classics): "the being blessed [*esser beato*] is founded on the act that seeth, not that which loveth, which after followeth." The stillness of perception precedes the "movement" of love; but both phases are modes of action.

But in his discussion of this matter in Chapter Nine (p. 365), Maritain writes:

> I would say that there is for creative intuition three different states, in consequence of the spiritual spheres in which it acts.
>
> In the spiritual sphere which is its own world—the creative night of the preconscious, nonconceptual life of the intellect—poetic intuition is in its pure, original, and native state, in its state of innocence and integrity, in its God-given state. And it passes into the work through the instrumentality of the *poetic sense*.

This, I take it, is that transition from the "act formed within the preconscious life of the intellect" to the moment when that inspiration is first consciously noted: Dante's "act that seeth." Maritain continues (p. 366):

Thus poetic intuition penetrates into the world of the early morning vision of the intellect, or of nascent logos. There, it is no longer in its connatural state, but in an alien state, peculiar to *the work as mentally conceived, the work as thought*. And then a certain objective virtuality which was contained in poetic intuition is, as it were, detached from it and brought to the act: poetic intuition passes into the work through the instrumentality of the *action* and the *theme*.

Notice that at this point he reserves the term "action" for *transitive* action—"motive" as one finds it in the play or poem. He is not thinking of the poet's being as act, nor of his initial act of perception, nor of the "act" he perceives. And Maritain proceeds to explain that the action itself (in this sense) may be developed "harmonically" to produce the larger forms of epic or novel. He writes (p. 369):

To sum up, I shall say that the poetic sense or inner melody, the action and the theme, the number or harmonic structure, are the epiphanies of poetic intuition or creative emotion passing into the work.

Maritain's elucidation of the roots of lyric, epic, and drama is of great value and originality. But I must leave that aside in order to follow the thin line of our reflections on "action," as Maritain relates that notion to poetry's new self-awareness. Does the modern lore correct, or supersede, the whole theory of poetry as action? If not, why does Maritain here in Chapter Nine present this newly-defined lyric awareness as more fundamental than action? There is great danger, at this point, of fatal blundering; let us note some of the reservations and distinctions with which Maritain has surrounded his account. For nowhere are his characteristic flexibility, tact, and intellectual humility more crucial; the reader must appreciate them if he is to avoid misunderstandings.

One must remember, first of all, that Maritain is talking

about the *Epiphanies* of creative intuition, i.e., the way it *appears* to the poet at successive stages of his work. He is concerned to safeguard the validity of the poet's *experience*, lest the whole notion of poetry-in-itself be lost. And he knows that the whole wisdom of modern art bids the poet, *qua* poet, take poetry as a jealous god. At the moment of poetry's first appearance he does not dare to be aware of anything but *it*. He must quiet the feelings, the senses, and the mind, lest his intuition vanish, leaving him with a mere dry bundle of concepts to show for his infidelity.

Moreover, Maritain never forgets that the crucial phase of the creative process is subconscious or preconscious. And he knows that a theory of subconscious life—whether his own Thomistic one, or Freud's—can never be based on direct evidence. It must depend on two things: a general conception of psychic life, and a study of such dreams, unwilled gestures, and inspirations as seem to emerge from the subconscious and enter the conscious mind. In Chapter Three, "The Preconscious Life of the Intellect," he takes account of the point of view, and some of the concepts and discoveries, of contemporary psychology. The reader should remember that discussion too, in thinking over the meaning of the "three epiphanies." It is of the essence of Maritain's method to adopt various points of view, and to exploit various terminologies, in order to reveal poetic intuition as it were "in the round." And he can do this only because he does not make a fetish of *any* formulation of the problem. His philosophical concepts and structures are always regarded as more or less inadequate means to the intellectual perception itself, and in this respect his work is closely analogous to that of the modern masters of art whom he so greatly admires.

Thus when in Chapter Nine he closely follows the experience of the poet, he does not intend, I think, to abandon the other perspectives he has presented, but rather to correct and

complement them. Nor does he ask the reader to do so. Thus
he is acutely aware of the dangers in the cult of poetry-in-itself
and in isolation; and he explores these dangers at length in
Chapter Five, "Poetry and Beauty," and in Chapter Seven,
"Poetic Experience and Poetic Sense." The new freedom of
poetry in the widest sense—freedom, like that of modern science, from the notion of Being—has proved to be as dangerous
as fission itself; perhaps more so, for the fission of the soul
concerns us more intimately than the fission of the physical
world. It is Maritain, as much as anyone, who has made us
aware of this. And that is why he keeps us reminded, throughout the book, that Poetry, wonderful as it is, is not God, but
only a gift dwelling most precariously in the human psyche.

If one tries to follow *The Three Epiphanies* with the relevant teachings of the whole book in mind, one can see that
the underlying vision of *poetando*, is (though many-sided) consistent. But a question remains, about the relation of poetic
intuition to action in the widest sense, which I think is particularly important in this generation. For it appears that
poetry's self-awareness is an achievement which is now complete. Can any poet hope to go farther, under this dispensation,
than Mallarmé and Valéry? Can anyone hope to achieve a
fuller awareness than is to be found in *Creative Intuition?* The
best contemporary poets, beginning with Eliot and including
Hart Crane (with whose frustrations this discussion began), are
looking for another way to understand poetry. And the question is, can they understand it as action without losing the
precious essence? I have tried to show that Maritain, with his
respect for the modern poet's experience, would doubt it. For to
see the successive phases of *poetando* as modes of action would
be to place it, at once, in a vast web of analogical relationships—between the poet and other beings; between his mortal
being and his vision, between his vision and the work in which
he embodies it. The poet's isolation would be gone: meanings

moral and metaphysical, historical and epistemological would appear. He would be freed from the freedom of poetry-in-itself —a "freedom" which now looks airless and dark—but would he survive *as poet* in such a naked condition of mortality?

This question may be understood both as theoretical and as practical. One may gather, I think, from Maritain's whole book that he would answer the theoretical question in the affirmative: it is possible to understand poetic intuition both as ultimate, "in itself," *and* as a mode of action. The chapter on *The Three Epiphanies* may be read that way. And in his superb section on Dante (p. 370) he shows that Dante in fact did this. Dante seems to have been able to see his inspiration from many sides, in the round, without violating it; and to develop it "harmonically" on the vastest scale, yet in obedience to its most intimate promptings. But Maritain leaves the practical question, whether a modern poet could entertain the perilous notion of action and survive as a poet, unanswered. He knows that Dante's world and Dante's kind of belief—to say nothing of his genius—are inaccessible to us. And he respects the uniqueness of individual experience and the mysteries of art too much to pronounce upon them in a practical way. One should try to emulate this wisdom and this humility: the crucial questions, questions of concrete reality, are beyond us.

The reader will have noticed that in questioning *Creative Intuition* I have skirted a great many interesting matters without going into them at all. That may suggest, I hope, the richness of the book. One might ask it many questions, and receive many luminous answers. There is no substitute for reading the book itself.

James's Dramatic Form

It has often been pointed out that Henry James's attempt to write for the theater marks an important turning point in his career. He had behind him a certain success as a writer of fiction, but this success had begun to wane. He felt that his aims as an artist were becoming clearer, but that his public was losing interest. After his experience with the theater he returned to the novel. But at the moment of writing his plays he could not see what form his work was to take, and he seems to have considered the possibility at least that it would be drama. He had followed the theater all his life, and was aware that his fiction approached the form and texture of drama. He envied Dumas and Labiche their secure possession of a stage, an audience, a "theater."

But the theater he had to write for was the British theater of the eighties. The well-made play of the Scribe tradition, lightened and sweetened to suit the taste of the theatergoers of Victorian London, held the stage. Drama was understood as a plot or machine for holding the attention of an audience for two hours, and then releasing it in a good humor. The great Francisque Sarcey wrote, "The audience is the necessary and inevitable condition to which dramatic art must accommodate its means. . . . From this simple fact we derive all the laws of the theater without a single exception." When James set out to write his comedies he put the problem to himself in exactly these terms: to accept that audience and learn to obey the laws derived from its habits and its taste. "The mixture," he wrote, "was to be stirred to the tune of perpetual motion and served, under pain of being rejected with disgust, with the time-honored bread-sauce of the happy ending."

This narrow and cynical conception of drama is of course "true" as far as it goes. It is a necessary condition of drama that it hold an audience. Yet on this basis we have no clue to the distinction between various dramatic genres, or even between drama and other devices for entertaining an audience in a theater. The notion goes back, I think, to the seventeenth century, when all the arts addressed themselves to a comparatively small and homogeneous society, the embodiment of all values and the arbiter of taste. The neoclassic theorists in their reading of Aristotle failed to notice the distinction between *mythos* and *praxis*, plot and action; they did not digest the Aristotelian notion of drama as the imitation of an action by means of plot. This left them without an explicit theory of the substance of drama, and hence with a purely mechanical and empirical idea of its form. They assumed that serious drama was substantially the conflict between love and honor, or passion and reason, or desire and duty. Subsequent generations of theatergoers were to lose their interest in this theme, but not their demand for entertainment. We have seen the tyranny of the consumer become as absolute in drama as in advertising, and the playwright study his trade in the same spirit as the layout man and copywriter.

James found no difficulty in learning the tricks of this trade, and he turned out four plays which are mechanically as neatly put together as one could wish. All four are perpetually agitated comedies, parlor games, the stakes "love" and money. At the beginning of each we are shown the characters paired off in a certain arrangement which is not quite satisfactory; by the end they have effected a shift into a new and happier pattern. The suspense, the speed of the story, and the succession of clear and stagey situations never flag for a moment. James had solved the problem which he as craftsman had set himself. But it was easy for him, as it is for us, to see why the experiment was not a success. It was not satisfactory to him because the nature of the form ruled out in advance any subject he would have been interested in trying to dramatize. He could only take a minor idea, he says, which, with the habit of small natures, proved thankless. It is too evident that he disliked his characters and that the happy ending offended his taste. This must all have been as puzzling and unsatisfactory to his audience as it was to him.

When he wrote the preface to the published plays he speculated a little ruefully about what the plays might have been. He thought that the tone of farce might have carried them off if the audience had not so inexorably demanded the "bland air of the little domestic fairy tale." In spite of his attempts at good nature, his plays do approximate now and then a cold, hard Johnsonian type of farce, based on flat external caricature, and boldly absurd situations—a form in which the mechanical ticking of the plot is part of the basic vision. I think it possible that if one produced a James play now in the costume of the eighties one might bring out this farce. Perhaps an audience would even accept it as a satirical picture of a society now safely remote.

He abandoned the stage, but without thinking that the drama or even the theater lacked the resources he required. It was rather that particular form of drama and that particular theater which baffled and thwarted him. As he turned away from the theater he wrote, "Give me an hour, just an hour; Dumas and Augier never lacked it, and it makes all the difference; and with it I shan't fear to tackle the infinite." It was about this time too that he wrote the article on Benoit Coquelin which contains the following fine description of that actor's art:

> Mr. Coquelin's progress through this long and elaborate part, all of fine shades and pointed particulars, all resting on the keenest observation as well as appealing to it, resembles the method of the psychological novelist who (when he is in as complete possession of his form as M. Coquelin of *his*) builds up a character, in his supposedly uncanny process, by touch added to touch, line to line, illustration to illustration, and with a vision of his personage breathing steadily before him.

When James embarked upon his last group of novels and his critical prefaces he was free to tackle the subject which really interested him. It was in the effort to "dramatize" this subject that he made his great discoveries in dramatic form and technique. It is true that by rejecting the theater as he found it he also rejected some of the limitations which any theater imposes upon drama: the strict time limits, and the obligation to maintain a certain rhythmic tension in the face of that impatient crowd of Sarcey's. He clearly luxuriates in this freedom, multiplying his discriminations, taking his time, putting out of patience a large group of readers who accuse him of verbosity and hairsplitting. His novels are not literally dramas. I am not even sure that the phrase "described dramas" is very accurate for them. Yet both the texture of the writing and the large outlines of the form are truly dramatic. And I wish to suggest that his ideas of form and of techniques of presentation throw at least as much light upon drama as upon fiction.

The critical prefaces have been carefully studied by Joseph Warren Beach, Percy Lubbock, R. P. Blackmur, and others with whose work I am less familiar. Thanks to their work many of James's technical notions have become generally available. In the following notes I have taken some of the ideas, and indicated how they might be applied to drama, and what basic conceptions of dramatic form they constitute.

"PICTURE AND SCENE"

Percy Lubbock makes much of the distinction between "picture" and "scene" which James mentions several times in his prefaces. He writes:

> It is the method of picture-making that enables a novelist to cover his great spaces of life and quantities of experience so much greater than any that can be brought within the acts of a play. . . . The limitation of drama is as obvious as its peculiar power. It is clear that if we wish to see an abundance and multitude of life we shall find it more readily and summarily by looking for an hour into a memory, a consciousness, than be merely watching the present event of an hour, however crowded. . . . But it needs a mind to create that vista.

A novelist may and often does break down and tell all, while a writer for the stage never can. In this sense the novelist commands a resource not available to the dramatist. But this resource, so conceived, James disdained. He felt how easily it degenerated into mere formless loquacity. He preferred to dramatize the picture too, by viewing it through a consciousness different from his own, that of a character in the drama. The method is that of the dramatist, and if you look at a drama which contains "great spaces of life and quantities of experience" you can see the dramatist employing it. Behind the chief characters in *Antony and Cleopatra, Troilus and Cressida, King Lear,* these great spaces extend, because the characters are aware of them. In the two hours of playing time of *Ghosts* Ibsen makes us feel many years of Mrs. Alving's life and experience by making the characters in their various ways feel them. Mr. Lubbock's analysis suffers throughout from his failure to understand the nature and scope of the stage medium. The actors are not there only to illustrate for us the facts of the story, but through their make-believe to create an imagined world for the eye of the mind to dwell upon. Good dramatic writing, like good acting, owes much of its quality to the establishment of these imagined perspectives behind and beyond the little figures on the boards.

THE FINE INTELLIGENCE AS "REFLECTOR" AND AS COMPOSITIONAL CENTER

James almost invariably used a fine intelligence to give us the clue to the other characters and to the issues and values of his dramas. It had to be a fine intelligence if it was to perceive what James wanted his audience to perceive through it, yet it could not be James himself, for then James would have been telling us *about* his subject instead of presenting it to us directly. The problem and the solution both belong to drama, and good drama is full of Jamesian "reflectors." Enobarbus in *Antony and Cleopatra* is one. In the first three acts he interprets Antony and Cleopatra for us. We come to depend on him for the clue even when we have the chief characters in the flesh before us. This function is very clear in Scene 13 of Act III, when Cleopatra receives Caesar's emissary and Antony has him whipped. Enobarbus not only shows us what to think of Antony and Cleopatra at various moments, he also sums up the impression of the whole scene for us several times and at the end. It is not too much to say that the scene is composed and pulled together for us in Enobarbus' consciousness of it. Shakespeare thus uses Enobarbus both as "reflector" and as "compositional center" for this scene.

These notions of the reflector, and of the fine intelligence as the center of composition, are as useful in the analysis of Chekov's or Congreve's plays as in the analysis of Shakespeare's. The practitioners of "well-made" drama, who usually conceive their subjects in terms of a single narrative line or a monolinear argument, the demonstration of a thesis, do not need the notion of the reflector. Any dramatist who conceives his subject in the round, capable of being looked at from various angles, needs and uses these devices. But it was James who defined them clearly.

SITUATIONS AS LAMPS OR REFLECTORS

James describes the structure of *The Awkward Age* as follows:

> I draw on a sheet of paper . . . the neat figure of a circle consisting of a number of small rounds disposed at equal distance about a central object. The central object was my situation, my subject in itself to which the thing would owe its title, and the small rounds represented so many distinct lamps, as I liked to call them, the function of each of which would be to light with all due intensity one of its aspects. . . . Each of my "lamps" would be the light of a single "social occasion" in the history and intercourse of the characters concerned and would bring out to the full the latent color of the scene in question and cause it to illustrate, to the last drop, its bearing on my theme.

In this passage the Jamesian conception of the "round" subject is very clear. He thinks of it as a metaphysical or moral entity rather than as a sequence of events. It is, I think, an Action in Aristotle's sense of the word. The distinction between plot and action thus reappears in James's analysis of form, and he is then able to think of the story, or plot or arrangement of incidents as a means to an end: the end of revealing the Action which is the subject of the play.

He points out that the "occasions" which make up *The Awkward Age* are in effect the acts of a play. They are very much like the acts of a Chekhov play. The reviewers of Chekhov have not yet seen that his plays are composed, not as stories, in which the chief point of interest is to find out "what happened," but as a series of social occasions each of which throws its light upon the central subject. *The Cherry Orchard,* for instance, has a minimum of story in this sense, but a maximum of subject. The first act is the occasion of the return of Mme. Ranevsky's party to the Cherry Orchard; the second, a dilatory gathering on a warm evening; the third a rather hysterical party; the fourth, the departure of Ranevsky and her family. Each of these occasions illumines a facet of the subject, or action, "to possess the Cherry Orchard." By the time we are through we have seen this action from various angles and on various levels; and the completing of this vision, rather than the overt event which ends the little thread of story, completes for us the play.

There is of course no contradiction between the use of an intelligence as reflector and the use of the situation as reflector. The intelligent character reflects the occasion, and the occasion throws its light upon the central subject.

JAMESIAN SUSPENSE

Though the story is never the main interest in James's late works, they are very carefully composed in the dimension of time, having a beginning, a development, and an end in temporal succession. As Joseph Warren Beach points out, this order is that of the reader's developing awareness of the subject. We are finding out, not what happened, but what the true values in the situation are. And this process of discovery is itself dramatized. Sometimes it is dramatized for us in the growing awareness of the fine intelligence at the center of the composition. Very often the development of the investigation is controlled by switching from one intelligence to another. And in addition we are led from one social occasion or scene to another, whose succession (as well as their relation to the central subject) is significant.

If you once grant at all the interest of the subject, the investigation becomes a very intense and exciting project. Mr.

Beach aptly compares this suspense to that of a well-planned
detective story, which is an investigation on another level. But
for some reason Mr. Beach seems to doubt that it is "dramatic."
There are many familiar dramas in which this type of
suspense (once James has made us aware of it) may be demonstrated. It is very instructive, for example, to notice how in
Hamlet our sense of the evil in Denmark is made to develop
as we feel it now from the point of view of the soldiers, now
from the point of view of the King, now from the point of view
of Polonius, and now from the point of view of Hamlet himself.
Perhaps the clearest example is *Oedipus the King*. This drama
is primarily an investigation; and though it has the swift movement and the "plot interest" of the mystery story, it is also an
investigation of the moral and metaphysical realities of Oedipus' situation. These interest the chorus even more deeply than
the question, Who killed Laius?

James Subject as a Static Composition

When we have taken, in succession, the points of view of
the various "reflectors," when we have seen the central intelligence, on various "occasions," complete its investigation, the
drama is over, and the subject is revealed as a static composition. In *The Golden Bowl*, for instance, Maggie Verver is
gradually revealed as the central intelligence. She understands,
at length, herself and all the other characters in relation to the
issues and the values of the action they have been through—
she gets at last the "truth" of their situation. In her awareness
and then in the mind's eye of the reader the whole comes to
rest, and is perceived as motionless, like the composed canvas
of a painter.

Mr. Beach has described the composition of James's later
novels in terms like these. He concludes that James's subject
is essentially plastic rather than narrative or dramatic. He
thinks that the narrative movement is lost in these later novels;

and though he feels that they are full of the sense of "dramatic struggle" he cannot quite explain to himself how, granted the static subject, drama can still be there. I should prefer to say that the late novels are narrative *and* dramatic *and* plastic. The heresy would be to insist on one aspect of their form to the exclusion of the others.

As for the painter, he also may compose with a temporal succession of perceptions in mind; he also has ways of guiding the eye of the spectator from element to element to the final "stasis of aesthetic pleasure."

The notion of drama as a static composition is not popular with modern writers on the subject. Yet in what other terms are we to describe the full stop, the final rest, with which a completely achieved drama ends? This moment or this aspect corresponds to the epiphany in Greek drama. In Euripides the epiphany is characteristically presented in plastic terms—an arrangement of properties and corpses, with a visible *deus ex machina*. In Sophocles, though there may be a significant grouping of the characters, in tableau form, at the end, the final synthesis is made in the mind of the chorus as it at last "sees the truth."

It is easy to see, after the event, why James never found a public stage for his drama. The first answer is of course that the established and recognized public stage was too limited and too hard to crack. If you then go on to study the drama in his best novels, you see that this drama, by its very nature, postulates an audience which doesn't exist, so to speak, in public; and that it is founded upon James's anomalous and unique traditionalism, which is also far removed from the public consciousness.

James's drama is that of a fine, perceptive spirit which endeavors to secure for itself the best that the world has to offer: "Life," at its sharpest point of intensity and awareness. This fine spirit is always dispossessed, even disembodied. There

is usually some circumstance to explain its having been de-
prived of life—an American upbringing, poverty, a fatal but
hidden disease. Some of James's critics have tried to explain
this deprivation in Freudian terms, as the result of some dis-
turbance in James's own emotional life. It is true that James
keeps sexual passion at the periphery of his consciousness; but
his drama is no more disembodied sexually than it is in a number of other ways. His attitude to sex may be a symptom rather
than a cause, and one can believe that if he had had a place
and a name, "sex" also would have been added unto him. However that may be, his fine spirits exist almost exclusively on the
plane of moral awareness and activity.

To "register" at all, they require therefore a stage, a setting,
a "theater" which is based upon and embodies their awareness.
James's fine spirits are usually American, but he hypostatizes
the setting as "Europe," as a drawing room, secure like Shaw's
drawing room, feeling eternal (so that even the Shavian bandits
drink tea at five)—but unlike Shaw's the epitome of culture
and the heir of the ages. Its architectural setting, its costume
and its custom, its taboos and its heirarchies, all of its forms,
embody the values the Jamesian Americans are seeking, and
above all the value of concrete embodiment itself. For James's
people, who must exist on what he called the "high plane,"
are extremely worldly, pagan, moral, and irreligious. The values
they seek are traditional, but a tradition which no longer in-
formed a society would be of no use to them whatever.

This drama is "dramatic" enough, even stagey, and James
always felt it to be so. It is not subjective or private, being in
the tradition of European moralists since the Greeks. But it is
difficult to make its elements visible to a modern audience.

I have remarked that Chekhov was no more interested
than James in the monolinear story or thesis, but saw his subject in the round; and that he evolved a form with many close
analogies to James's. He also assumed a society—or rather (the

distinction is important) found one—and stuck close to it. He was in this the physician rather than the moralist; he took the people, the themes and the situations he found around him. The material of his art was what his audience was already prepared to recognize, whereas a large part of James's ingenuity is spent in making the elements of his composition visible at all. Chekhov's people are perhaps more lost than James's, but being lost in the flesh and the feelings, they are not lost to public view. If James had known Chekhov he would probably have felt that he had "lapsed to passivity from the high plane."

James did know Ibsen's plays, and was among the first in London to recognize his mastery as a dramatist. The plays of Ibsen's naturalistic period start, like James's own comedies, with Scribe, and it is possible to read them as social theses or as well-constructed stories. But his plays are composed on a deeper level also. He is neither sociologist nor entertainer, but, like James, a moralist. James recognized this also, but with mixed feelings. In Ibsen's plays, he wrote, "the lamp of the spirit burns as in tasteless parlors with the flame practically exposed." He may have been remembering the America he left, which must have been similar in many ways to Ibsen's Norway. James could no more accept Ibsen's Norway as real and ultimate than he could the America of the seventies. Ibsen's characters are not trying to realize a life of the spirit in any sort of traditional cultivated society; it is doubtful whether, in their gloomy quests, they envision the possibility of *any* "life," and certainly they are unaware of a traditional wisdom that could have anything to say to them. James complains that Ibsen's dramas always end at the point where the true interest and the true comedy of things should begin. And I think one can see that if Rosmer and Rebecca, for example, had married under the eyes of a group of interested and intelligent friends, instead of jumping into the millrace together, a truly "bristling" Jamesian subject would have resulted. But at the same moment Ibsen would have lost his audience. The plays which do end on such a note, *The Lady from the Sea, Little Eyolf*, are still the least esteemed of all Ibsen's dramas.

Did James ever think that British society actually provided the setting and the awareness he needed? Probably not; certainly not for long—his early letters seem to show that clearly. He willingly admitted that his people were too intelligent and too gifted to be probable. Their ideal social intercourse was derived from James's experience of society, but eventually became almost independent of it. He seems to have been moving toward an unrealistic theatrical convention, based on the rules and the tensions of politeness; the kind of convention which makes possible a Bérénice, a Hippolyte, an Alceste, a Millamant. Such a "stage" was a fundamental postulate of his inner life and of his art, and even in the semiretirement of his last period he continued to live up to its ghostly urbanity and agility. It is this which makes his prose so entirely unlike that of Proust or Virginia Woolf. Though he left society, he clung to its values; and while Proust recorded the dissolution of the moral being, James, with his shadow-boxing, kept in excellent trim.

The drama that James knew did not survive the last war. The most interesting writers for the stage between 1918 and 1939—among whom I should include Yeats, Eliot, Cocteau, Obey, Lorca—start completely afresh. The influences of the Moscow Art Theater, the Ballet, and the Music Hall, combine to produce a new conception of the theatrical medium. Not only nineteenth-century naturalism, but most European drama back through the seventeenth century, is explicitly rejected in favor of medieval farce, Greek tragedy, peasant rituals, and entertainments. The new dramatists are likely to be interested in religion, in myth, and in types of symbolism designed to reach a popular audience. Most of them would I think approve of Cocteau's description of *poésie de théâtre* as like the cordage of a ship—a composition of large coarse elements easily perceptible at a distance. Their estrangement from the prewar audience—if indeed it still exists—is complete. They neither ask for the support of the carriage trade, nor try, like James, to build a notion of the ideal cultivated spectator into their theatrical forms. The traditions and the symbols they like antedate the founding of the drawing room. It is not yet clear whether this strategy is any less desperate than James's. The vision they get of a drama speaking directly to the population in simple, ancient, fundamental terms, is perhaps a flattering illusion, like that of the mythical drowning man who sees his whole life before him at the moment of going under for the last time. Paris in the twenties is already far away, and we see now some of the dangers in the new line. One needs, I think, to place against Cocteau's theatrical virtuosity, and Eliot's abstract theological framework, and Lorca's luxuriant popular imagery, the Jamesian and classic conception of an Action, seen in the round, seen from many angles. James paid dearly for his position above the battle, but he found there some curiously universal technical concepts, useful in contexts he never dreamed of; and a conception of dramatic form which we still need if we are to see the drama of his time and ours in the right perspective.

The *Divine Comedy* as a
Bridge Across Time

The title of this essay is intended to suggest the fact that, though Dante was born seven hundred years ago in another country, he speaks to us here and now, with extraordinary intimacy and directness, in his great poem. Shelley's phrase for the *Divine Comedy*, a "bridge across time," is even more significant now than it was when Shelley first used it, both because another century and a half has passed, and because many more readers have learned to see the *Commedia* as Shelley did.

There have been at least *some* zealous readers of Dante ever since the *Commedia* first appeared. He suffered a partial eclipse during the seventeenth and eighteenth centuries, for that was a time when men tended to feel that their own enlightened age had all the answers, and that a medieval poet, with his "Gothic" obscurities and superstitions, could not possibly have much to offer them. But toward the end of the 18th century, the beginning of our own more faithless and dissatisfied period—the "age of revolutions" as it has been called —Dante began coming slowly into focus again. His fame, and the numbers of readers who understand and enjoy him, have been increasing faster and faster ever since, if we are to measure such things by the number of new editions and translations, and the number of new books *about* Dante, that have appeared in our time.

There is something rather paradoxical about Dante's increasing appeal to the modern world. The stupendous growth of science, technology and industry since the eighteenth century carries us farther and farther away from the comparatively cozy little world that Dante knew. Why, then, should so many readers, of so many different kinds, have discovered Dante during the last hundred and fifty years? A romantic, revolutionary spirit like Shelley turned to him with enthusiasm; so did a Harvard professor, our own Henry Wadsworth Longfellow. Cranks of many kinds try to use him for their purposes, as they do the Bible and Shakespeare. But, what is more significant, he feeds the intellectual life of our time through many channels. Historians read him in order to understand the roots of our tradition. Writers like the Thomas Mann of *The Magic Mountain*, or the Joyce of *A Portrait of the Artist as a Young Man* and *Ulysses*, find clues to their own themes and literary techniques in the *Commedia*. A list of modern poets who owe something to Dante would include many great names, not only in Italy but in Germany, England, and America. Among Americans, the late T. S. Eliot has been the most famous and influential follower of Dante. Eliot's poetry, even more than his critical studies, I think, continues to make Dante a living presence among us.

I realize that it would be impossible to discuss the importance that Dante actually has for so many poets, thinkers and scholars. The topic would be too vast, even for someone who knew enough; it would take more than the length of one essay to do justice to Dante's importance for *one* of the writers I mentioned. So I decided to interpret my assignment in a different way. What are some of the properties of the *Divine Comedy* that lead so many to read it now? What are some of the relevant insights that modern readers find there? What is

there about the poetry itself that makes it legible after so many
centuries—for us, as for Shelley, a "bridge across time?" Of
course such questions as these are not to be answered in a brief
essay. But, at least, in considering them, one can sample bits
of the great poem itself. And I suppose that, in writing about
Dante, the point is always to get as close as one can to his
own creation.

To begin with, one must remember that Dante intended
the *Commedia* to answer practically all the questions that a
puzzled human being may ask himself in any generation. For
this purpose he starts, as everyone knows, with the experience
of being lost. The famous lines at the very beginning of the
poem allude to a recognizable moment of terror and bewilder-
ment. I quote, as always in this essay, from the literal prose
translation of Carlyle-Wicksteed:

> In the middle of the journey of our life
> I came to myself in a dark wood
> where the straight way was lost.*

We soon see, if we read on, that he was more thoroughly lost
than most of us have the energy to be: lost in his emotional
and moral life, lost in the jungle of contemporary politics,
caught in the philosophical and religious issues of his time.
And from the dark wood of this life he is led by Virgil straight
into Hell itself, the fictive realm beyond the grave where he
meets the spirits of so many who had been completely and
irremedably lost in their lives on earth.

Modern readers have no difficulty whatever with the *Inferno;* it seems to speak our language. That is partly because
of the vitality of the great lost souls like Farinata, or Brunetto
Latini, or Ulysses, or Ugolino. Probably the lost lovers, Paolo
and Francesca, are the most famous. "Always on opening the

---

* Dante Alighieri, *The Divine Comedy: The Carlyle-Wicksteed
Translation* (New York: The Modern Library, 1950).

book," says Pirandello, "we shall find the living Francesca confessing her sweet sin to Dante, and if we return a hundred thousand times in succession to reread that passage, a hundred thousand times in succession Francesca will utter words, never repeating them mechanically, but speaking them every time for the first time with such a living and unforeseen passion that Dante, each time, will swoon when he hears them." Pirandello describes very accurately the effect we get from the lost spirits in the *Inferno*, and his remarks also throw light on his own art. The characters in his epoch-making play, *Six Characters in Search of an Author*, are caught in their destinies like Dante's lost souls, and the nightmare film of their lives is played over and over in the same way, with no change or hope of change. The visible scenes of the *Inferno*, like its people, have also proved to be uncannily familiar to the inhabitants of the modern megalopolis: the towers of the city of Dis, for example, glowing red through the smog, or the restless, anonymous crowds, "so many, I had not thought death had undone so many," as Eliot puts it in the first section of the *Wasteland*, echoing a line from the third canto of the *Inferno*. Sartre, Brecht, Pound, Mann, are among the twentieth-century writers who have envied Dante his hellish effects, and carefully studied his poetic and dramatic techniques in order to learn how to represent our modern world as they see and feel it.

Virgil, Dante's beloved guide, defines Hell as the "place" of those "who have lost the good of the intellect"—not the intellect itself, for Hell is full of intellectuals—but the *good* of the intellect. Dante explores in detail the human condition when the mind, ingenious and vigorous though it may be, has missed the sense of its own true welfare. But in the great plan of the *Commedia* as a whole the *Inferno* is only an extended prologue, like the sinister and portentous situation presented at the beginning of a classical tragedy. It is the necessary preliminary to the triumphant quest of the *Purgatorio* and the *Paradiso*. As soon as Dante and Virgil emerge from the dead air of Hell, and respond to the beauty of dawn on the beach at the foot of the Mount of Purgatory, the intellect begins to revive with the senses. Slowly, as the travellers proceed, answers to the moral, the political-historical, and the religious questions, which Dante had despaired of answering in Hell and in the dark wood, appear, in all that he sees and hears on the Mountain, and especially in what Virgil tells him. The *Purgatorio* and *Paradiso* unfold the meaning of human life in the light of Dante's long Hebraic-Christian and Classical tradition. Here the question of the relevance of the *Commedia* becomes more difficult. Why does his exploration of the world of his tradition, the complex order that the Middle Ages discerned in human affairs and in the cosmos, mean any more to us than an imaginative travelogue in a long-lost allegorical convention?

The modern world, needless to say, knows infinitely more history, biology, physics, and astronomy than the fourteenth century did. At the same time we believe much less—if, indeed, belief in Dante's sense exists at all in our time. Nevertheless Dante's great vision of order does speak to us, and it does so, I think for two main reasons. The first has to do with the dramatic and dialectical nature of his poetry; he presents his ideas with extraordinary sophistication and realism. The second reason is that many of Dante's ancient ways of understanding man and his world seem to be immune to time; they are not superannuated by the changes that science and technology bring with such bewildering speed. I will try to explain what I mean by that point first.

Take, for example, Dante's cosmos, which is that of Ptolemaic astronomy. The sphere of the earth is motionless, in that scheme, at the center of the universe; the planets, the sun, and the stars move around it in intricate seasonal and diurnal patterns. This picture has of course been out of date for hundreds of years; no modern schoolboy could take it seriously. But it is adequate enough so that Dante can use it to tell time. Moreover, when he can see the sky again, after hell, and he notices Venus, near dawn, very bright on the horizon; or during the second night on the Mountain sees the moon, retarded almost to midnight, making the stars appear more thin to us in its bright light, he can make us see just what he sees. That is the great advantage which his human-sized little cosmos has over the shifting theories of modern astronomy: it is visible, we can confirm it, in a way, by taking a look at it ourselves. We tell ourselves that we can't believe in it, that modern astronomers, none of whom would dream of putting our tiny speck of earth anywhere near the center of their schemes, are finding out what the universe is really like. But unless we are very accomplished mathematicians we have to take that largely on faith; it is all most of us can do to decipher third-hand, and most probably misleading, accounts of the latest theories. Meanwhile we continue to see the sun rise in the east and set in the west just as Dante did.

Considerations of the same sort apply to Dante's conceptions of history and of the ideal order of human society. The human world that he was aware of was much smaller than ours, in both its temporal and its spatial dimensions. His notion of history is based on the Bible and a few Greek and Roman authors, and his theories of government are devised to make sense out of fourteenth-century European politics. Neither Asia, Africa, nor the undiscovered Americas entered into his calculations. But he was driven by the stubborn faith that there must be some way for the political animal to get his bearings in history, and to run his community in accord with reason and nature; and so he digs down to certain perennial human needs or aspirations. In his prose work on political theory, *De Monarchia,* he tells us that society must be based on law and reason; it must have a single ruler whose duty it is to serve law and reason; the secular and ecclesiastical authori-

ties must be separate: there must be a world government.
Dante's theory is a combination of Greek, mostly Aristotelian,
political philosophy, with religious and historic notions derived
from the Hebraic-Christian tradition, and it helps one to understand European ways of thinking about the human community
through Shakespeare's history plays, at least, even though the
international authority of the Empire was already being super-
seded by independent kingdoms in Dante's own day. *De
Monarchia* is read in our day, however, not only as a clue to
European history, but as a classic of political theory.

In the *Commedia* Dante's conceptions of history and society emerge gradually, in many different contexts, and in response to questions that occur to the traveller beyond the grave.
The spirits he meets tell him their brief and poignant life
stories, and from them we get a picture of the chaos of Italy.
The traveller, as he reaches Purgatory, begins to wonder why
his country is so torn, and whether any cure is conceivable.
Halfway up the Mountain he meets Marco Lombardo in the
bitter smoke where the angry try to rid themselves of that vice.
Marco was angry on earth, where he fought in vain for the
right as he saw it, and here in the world of the dead he is
angry still, especially when he remembers the pugnacity, stub-
borness, and blindness he had suffered in life. He briefly informs
Dante that Church and State must be recognized as two quite
independent authorities if Italy is ever to know peace, and the
myopic conflicts between Emperor and Pope, both claiming all
authority, ever be brought to an end. It is Marco who presents
the charming image of the eager but fallible human soul as a
child—the premise of all theories of government and education:

> From his hand who fondly loves her
>> before she is in being, there issues, like a child
>> playing, weeping, and laughing,
> The simple little soul that knows nothing,
>> except that, moved by a joyful maker,

> she turns all willingly to what delights her.
> First she tastes the savor of a trifling good:
> there she is beguiled, and runs after it,
> if guide or bridle does not turn her love aside.
> Therefore it is necessary to place laws as a bridle;
> it is necessary to have a ruler who might discern
> the towers, at least, of the true city.

The smoke of anger, memories of the state of Dante's beloved Italy, Marco Lombardo's noble and troubled spirit, his picture of the childlike soul entering the world, make a resonant context for the notion of separation of Church and State which, in *De Monarchia*, is set forth at much more length in Dante's sober prose. In the *Commedia* all of Dante's ideas of order in human affairs and in the cosmos are presented as the traveller grasps them in particular contexts; and the farther he goes the better does he grasp the basic notions. Thus when Dante reaches Paradise he will hear the spirit of Justinian himself expound human government and its history, and then he will understand what Marco told him so briefly in a far wider and clearer perspective.

I have said that Dante's notions about the world are significant still; but his vision of the human psyche itself, as it explores every realm of experience, is much more significant. Dante's own spirit, as it moves toward more and more comprehensive concepts of order, is the protagonist of the entire poem. In Hell Dante is drawn into the hopeless sufferings and endlessly repeated motives of the lost, but when he emerges and starts up the Purgatorial Mountain, he slowly becomes aware of the processes of intellectual growth in his own being. Many writers, artists, and researchers in science and mathematics have acutely observed, and recorded for *us*, the stages of the creative process in themselves; and educators of insight, beginning with Socrates, have studied out the steps of the learning process. But none, so far as I know, can give us as much insight into the growth of the mind and the spirit as Dante does in the *Purgatorio*. During the daylight hours the Pilgrim climbs, sees, talks, thinks, and learns from Virgil's explanations; during the three nights of the journey he must pause, rest, sleep, and dream, in the hope of new inspirations to help him on his way. Within this natural rhythm one can learn to see Dante's spirit moving in many ways from fact to understanding; from what only the physical eye sees to what the mind grasps in its wider focus; from abstract formulas to the realities behind them—in short, from the Letter to the Spirit, as Dante himself might have put it: from the "letter" that "killeth" to the "spirit" that "giveth life."

Dante knew exactly where the central life of his great poem was. In the *Letter* dedicating the *Paradiso* to his patron, Can Grande, he says that "Man, as by good or ill deserts, in the exercise of the freedom of his choice, he becomes liable to punishing or rewarding justice," is the subject of the *Commedia*, underlying the whole fictive journey beyond the grave. The human spirit as it finds or loses its way is the basis of the poem, more fundamental than the cosmic setting, beautiful and revealing though that is; more fundamental, even, than the philosophy of history and society. It is Dante's lore of the intimate life of the psyche that can teach us most now. And it is his subtle, candid, and direct awareness of the spirit's ceaseless quests and longings that makes him the *poet* he is; "I am one who, when love breathes in me, take note, and in that mode which he dictates within, go signifying," as he tells his rival poet, Bonagiunta, who has asked him for the formula of his style.

This brings me to the second and most important reason for Dante's life in our time: his poetry, and his very deep understanding of the poetic art.

When Eliot was first writing about Dante, more than forty years ago, he found it necessary to point out that the *Com-*

media is poetry, even though it employs the methods of medieval allegory, even though it sometimes goes into long philosophical and theological expositions. Thanks partly to Eliot, one can now say that the *Commedia* reaches us simply because it *is* poetry: it is written in that mysterious, supra-temporal *lingua franca* that great poets, since Homer, speak as their native language. When Juliet, in her moonlit balcony, confesses her love to Romeo, we do not have to demand Shakespeare's credentials, or enquire whether he had been in Verona that night: we recognize some sort of truth directly in Juliet's words. And when Piccarda, in the milky substance of the moon, tells Dante, "It is the property of *caritas* to still our wills," we do not ask ourselves how he got to the moon so long before our sputniks. Piccarda's words themselves "ring a bell"—at least they do if there is something in the reader's own experience for them to strike on. We get the meaning and the "truth" of poetry when we recognize, however unexplicitly, the experience it embodies.

Dante was more sharply aware than most poets of this limitation of poetry. He did not have the illusion that his poetry could replace first-hand experience; he knew that he must always appeal to what his readers had themselves felt and perceived. When he came to write the *Paradiso* he faced, therefore, his most difficult problem as poet, because his experiences of the heavenly vision were so rare and so evanescent. In the *Paradiso* he spent all his technical resources as poet, and at the same time was most scrupulous in not pretending to do more than poetry *can* do. The opening sequences of the heavenly journey are therefore one of the best places to study Dante's conception of poetry. It is there that he lets us know what poetry *can* and what it *cannot* do.

At the top of the Mount of Purgatory, when the traveller is being made ready to rise to the stars, he has to drink first of the stream of Lethe, which makes him forget all the evil he has known, and then of Eunoe, whose waters restore all memory of good. So Dante lets us know, by means of these two magical streams, that the heavenly vision will not be a matter of "seeing life steadily and seeing it whole," but of concentrating on one strictly limited aspect of experience. We must turn away from most of what we have known, and grope about in whatever small heavenly feelings we may have had, if we are to get the clue to the last Canticle.

As he rises unbelievably into the starry sky with Beatrice, he puts his poetic problem with his usual concision:

> Gazing on her, such I became within
>   as Glaucus was, tasting the grass
>   that made him sea-fellow of the other gods.
> To pass beyond humanity could not be told in
>   words; therefore let this example suffice him
>   for whom grace reserves the *experience*.

Nothing that he can say will avail, if the reader has not, by the grace of God, had such an experience. But he can tell us where to look for possible traces of analogous feelings in ourselves, and also where *not* to look, for he knows first-hand how hard it is to hold the proper focus. Even when he gets to the moon, in the third canto, he cannot believe in the first blessed spirits who appear there:

> So did I behold many a contenance, eager to speak;
>   whereupon I fell into the error opposite
>   to the one that kindled love between the man and the fountain.
> No sooner was I aware of them,
>   thinking them reflected images,
>   than I turned my eyes to see of whom they were;
> and saw nothing, and turned them forward again
>   straight into the light of my sweet guide,
>   who smiling glowed in her sacred eyes.
> "Do not wonder that I smile,"
>   she said, "at your childlike thought,
>   since it does not yet trust its foot upon the truth,
> but turns you, as usual, to vacancy."

The man who loved the fountain is, of course, Narcissus, doting on his own reflection in the water. It is natural for Dante, as it is for us, to mistrust beatitude, and to assume that heavenly intuitions are nothing but narcissism. But Beatrice shows him that in this realm of experience the heart's desire is objectively *there.*

At the beginning of the second canto Dante, as poet of the *Paradiso,* directly warns the reader:

> O you, who are there in your little boat,
>   longing to listen, following my way
>   behind my timbers singing as they go,
> turn back to visit your own shores again:
>   do not trust to the open sea, for perhaps,
>   once losing me, you would be left astray.

I do not suppose that we could follow him with the faith he wanted his readers to share. But if we take care not to lose him, we can see, reflected in his own mind and feelings, the deepest needs of the human spirit spread out through the nine heavens.

The *Inferno* shows the human spirit "as" lost; the *Paradiso* shows it "as" reaching its ultimate fulfillment. Dante knows that he and his readers can only get one aspect of human experience into focus at once, and he is always careful to define *that* focus, to let us know what angle of vision, and what mode of feeling, constitute each stage of the long journey from the dark wood to the summit of heaven. In this he is as scrupulous as a modern scientist, who offers his results not as total and final truth, but as defined by a certain working hypothesis and a certain experimental apparatus. It is this scrupulous awareness of the nature and source of his poem-making that enables us to read Dante with confidence, whatever we may believe or disbelieve. And it is the same quality that leads so many contemporary writers in search of a more conscious poetic technique to study the *Commedia.*

I have one more small point to make about Dante's poetic art before I conclude my observations.

In the dark wood, when Dante first meets the spirit of Virgil "hoarse with long silence," he cries to him, "May the long study and the great love, which made me search through your book, avail me." His love and study of Virgil's book, the *Aeneid*, do avail him: Virgil's spirit revives in that warmth and light, speaks, leads him on the long path to freedom and sanity. In the middle of Hell, in the sad and restless domain of the Sodomites, Dante meets his old teacher, Brunetto Latini, and tells him that he will always remember

> The dear and good fatherly image of you, when in the world,
> hour by hour, you taught me how man makes himself eternal.

We are not accustomed to thinking that the patient study of long-dead authors could make a man eternal, but Dante, like many other men in the early Renaissance, did think so. One of the themes that runs through the *Commedia*, especially the *Purgatorio*, is that of the communion of poets from different places and different periods of the world's history. Disembodied and ghostly this communion may be, but it transcends time, some sort of life flickers across the ages; and so those who partake of the timeless life of poetry may be called "eternal" themselves.

The last point that I wish to make about Dante's poetic art is that he very consciously intended it to transcend the provincialities of time and place in this way. He thought he had learned the poetic art, in part at least, from Latin poets who had died more than a thousand years before his time. He thought that he thereby shared both their art and their vision. And he confidently aimed his own poetry into a future which he could not possibly have imagined. That is one reason why he *does* "bridge time" for us—reaching us from fourteenth-century Florence, carrying us all the way back to the Old Testament and the Greeks, where our tradition has its sources.

I have not even tried to discuss Dante's actual importance in the modern world, to which so many men, in so many ways, and in so many countries, now testify. I have tried, instead, to suggest, very briefly, some of the ways in which the vision and the art of the *Commedia* reaches us here and now. But of course this topic also has no end. Even in my time the *Commedia*, thanks to the patient labors of its admirers, has revealed new beauties and new insights; it is always renewing its vitality in our actual world. Who could hope, even with the requisite erudition, to expound that in one essay? Or who could predict what the next generation, or the generation after that, will find in the *Commedia*? All that one can really say with any confidence is that it continues to unfold for us, and for that we must simply be very grateful.

Molière

"Englishmen, have always loved Molière," said Lytton Strachey. The same may be said of Americans and Germans, of Russians and Italians and Spaniards. For Molière is the most universally intelligible of all the great artists who form our image of the human animal. He has the divine gift of making men laugh in any language and in any period, even our own rather morose one. His comic sequences have the formal beauty of music or ballet; his art has an axiomatic quality, which makes it as fresh, inevitable and surprising as the truth. When we read his plays or see them on the stage we feel that his common sense, the basis of his laughter, really is common to civilized mankind, and therefore humane in the best sense of the word. The absurd, logical and delightful world of his theater is always there, whenever we look at it: a bright spot in our troubled awareness of the human, with the charm, and the rare value, of sanity.

Molière's comedies are in their very essence theatrical, but they come alive on the printed page for any reader with a little willingness to make-believe. For all their clarity, however, we cannot really explain their magic: Molière is ultimately as enigmatic as any genius. Yet one may come to know him intimately as one learns to know a friend or a piece of music. And for this purpose it helps to know something about his theater; some of the ways in which his art has been understood and enjoyed in different periods, and the main facts of his life, which partakes of the gusto and gallantry of the comedies themselves.

MOLIÈRE'S LIFE

Molière (whose real name was Jean-Baptiste Poquelin) was born in Paris in 1622, of a substantial bourgeois family. His father was an upholsterer, and a man of some importance, for he was upholsterer to the King: *tapissier du roi.* The elder Poquelin was thus able to secure the wordly advantages for his children, and young Molière was sent to the fashionable Jesuit school of Clermont, where he studied from 1635 to 1641. The Jesuits gave him the good classical education of the time, which included a study of the Roman comic authors Terence and Plautus. The Jesuits used the theater in their educational scheme, and it is believed that Molière was taught to perform Roman comedy while still in school. At Clermont he also made "good connections," as boys are supposed to do still when their fathers spend money on their education. Thus Molière found himself, from the very first, in the middle of French life, in the healthy growing time of the great age of Louis XIV.

Molière's father expected him to carry on the family business, but Molière became interested in the theatrical profession through the Béjart family. The Béjarts were also *bourgeois de Paris,* but they were interested in the arts; they had a touch of what was later to be called Bohemianism. Madeleine Béjart became Molière's mistress; later in life he married Armande Béjart, her daughter by another man. Molière seems to have had the usual dispute with his father about his choice of profession, but Poquelin senior relented in time, and helped his son out with money for his theatrical ventures.

Molière's first attempts were with the Béjarts in Paris. But their "Illustre Théâtre," as they called it, was a financial failure. They abandoned Paris, and from 1646 to 1658 Molière with several members of the Béjart family toured the provinces with a small acting company. This was Molière's fertile apprenticeship as actor-manager, and as author also, for his first farces were written in this period. He acquired his sure knowledge of the public, and his extraordinary mastery of the stage itself, in the only way, the hard way. Our information on this period is not extensive or certain, but we are safe in imagining Molière working very hard, suffering the risks and disappointments of the profession, reaching, at last, success and prosperity, and all the while taking his share of the pleasures of this life. It has often been pointed out that he was the unmarried leader of a troupe with several attractive women in it, and that he was by nature "very amorous."

In 1658 Molière moved his company to Paris under the patronage of the Court. *The Highbrow Ladies* was presented in 1659. It is, among other things, a humorous picture of the literary ladies of the Hôtel de Rambouillet. It delighted Paris— all but the Hôtel de Rambouillet—and its success assured his place in the capital. From that time until his death in 1673 his plays followed one another with great rapidity.

In Paris, between the city and the Court, in the center of the power and culture of all France, Molière's life was lived in public, and a great deal is known about his last fourteen years, the summit of his career. He had an unparalleled opportunity to live and to observe the life of "man in society." No wonder he worked with such speed to catch the fascinating image in the mirror of his comedy. But his position was extremely perilous, maintained only by ceaseless fighting. Every play he produced had to please the audience, if he was to support his players. The King helped him, but not enough to make his company independent of their city following. Each of his own plays had to be defended from the machinations of those who felt attacked: *Tartuffe*, for instance, from many implacable churchmen, and *The Highbrow Ladies* from the literary coteries. Molière had very thorny relations, all this time, with his rivals and his colleagues, notably Racine and the composer Lully. He was always obliged to cultivate the King, who was his friend from the first, but required frequent doses of flattery. His marriage with Armande Béjart, with whom he was deeply in love but who was almost young enough to have been his daughter, was full of suffering.

All of this and much more is known about the troubles of Molière's illustrious career in Paris, and his admirers often seek the clue to the depth of his comedy in Molière's own sufferings. But that lively spirit never wore his heart on his sleeve, either in his writings or in his life. His public controversies reveal his pleasure in combat, his wit, objectivity, and balanced intelligence, but no bitterness or self-pity. His life, like his art, was based upon the kind of self-evident truth which may be made publicly clear. Purely private troubles, others' or his own, he disregarded. He was playing the title role in the last, and one of the greatest, of his comedies, *The Imaginary Invalid,* two hours before he died of a disease, probably tuberculosis, which was not imaginary. Molière and his real disease have departed, but his imagined invalid lives on, to our perennial delight.

Molière's Theater

I have remarked that Molière's theater has proved both intelligible and delightful to all civilized mankind. At the same time it is, of course, extremely French. It has that alert and wordly pep which is properly called the *esprit gaulois.* Rabelais revealed it before Molière, and so did the late medieval farces which prepared his way on the French stage. This spirit still lives so unmistakably among the French that one is tempted to say Molière created it in the forms we know, instead of merely expressing it. And yet his theater, in its essential humanity and its peculiar charm, floats free, alive beyond his time and race.

The charm of Molière's theater is not the charm of his characters, if one thinks of them as real people. Molière off stage was probably fond of young lovers, and of the formidable race of serving-maids who castigate their masters with such frank enjoyment. But in his theater these types are to be laughed *at* as well as *with:* they are seen in the same clean, steady light as his hypocrites, hypochondriacs, and social climbers. Molière never tries to ingratiate himself with the luxury market through the glamour of tweeds, Scotch, and an insolent Junior League drawl, like the writers of our advertisements and light comedies. His lightness is of a different order. He is addressing the impersonal and disinterested good sense which no income group, class, or individual owns: the sanity of humanity at large. "I beg you to learn, Marquis," he wrote in *La Critique de l'École des Femmes,* "that good sense has no fixed place in the theater, and that the difference between a *louis d'or* and fifteen *sols* has nothing to do with good taste." In the light of this good sense, all of his characters are comic, and the charm is in the whole lively scene.

Molière flattered no one but the King, who was both his good friend and the official recipient of literary adulation. But he offended many in his audiences who could not get his humorous perspective and thought they recognized their own portraits on his stage. This was not his intention, any more than flattery was. "Nothing displeases him so much as being accused of intending particular people in the portraits he makes," he has Brecourt say of himself in *L'Impromptu de Versailles;* "his purpose is to picture manners without touching individuals, and all the characters he represents are characters in the air, phantoms really, which he dresses according to his whim to delight the audience."

When one considers the Paris of Louis XIV, that dangerous focus of vanity, envy, and the thirst for power, it seems almost miraculous that Molière should have been able to put his free and clear-eyed comedy there, in the very center—and even make the public laugh at the mirror image he showed it. "C'est une étrange entreprise que de faire rire les honnêtes gens," he remarked with characteristic humor and courage: "It is a strange project—to make the honest laugh." Strange indeed: for the people Molière wanted to make laugh were no more honest than we are, before they saw his show. It is his own sturdy faith in common sense which creates the ideal audience, makes it honest, and makes it laugh. We can know this, whether Molière did or not, for his comedy has this effect upon us: our laughter makes us, for the moment, humane. This, I suppose is the mysterious property of much great comedy, but especially of Molière's.

It helps one to appreciate the peculiar quality of this theater—the sharpness of its characters, which so often dismayed the contemporary audience, combined with their impersonal, abstract, legendary scope—if one remembers that it was the outgrowth of an ancient popular tradition, that of the Commedia dell'Arte. The Commedia spread from Italy all over Europe in the late Renaissance, revivifying the theater, giving the great dramatists of the seventeenth century—Shakespeare and Molière among them—their opportunity, much of their theatrical skill, and much of their material. The players of the Commedia improvised their words and performances on the basis of familiar scenarios, often derived from Roman comedy: stock intrigues, and broad comic situations which skilled performers could build on. Each of the players was professionally identified with a traditional character, or "mask": Harlequin, Pantalone (the rich old man) or the Doctor of Bologna (the classic stage pedant). This theater lived only in performance, since it was improvised. But we still sense its

vitality and glamour in contemporary accounts of the performances, in pictures of the players from Callot to Tiepolo,
and in the traces it left in dramatic literature.

Molière began to absorb the Commedia as a child in Paris,
watching the Italian players. When he went into the theater
himself, he took lessons from one of the masters, Tiberio Fiorilli,
and there is a picture of him, which is often published, imitating a dancelike gesture of Fiorilli's Scaramouche. From his
earliest farces to his last play, *The Imaginary Invalid*, the
great tradition of the Commedia lives in Molière's works.

"The types of the Commedia," M. Ramon Fernandez wrote
in his excellent *Vie de Molière*, "come down to us, thanks to
their masks, their costumes and their gestures, endowed with
an individuality which is both typical and concrete, very much
like that of the animals in the Fables. . . . If it is true that
a dramatic poet must base his creations upon creations which
are collective and anonymous, the Commedia can explain (in
part, of course) the marvellous sharpness of Molière's creations.
Thanks to it, seventeenth-century comedy had a mythology,
not literary like tragic mythology, but alive and real." The
comic mythology of the Commedia helps one to understand
Molière's own description of his characters as "phantoms to
delight the audience." His old men tormented by young women,
his pedants with their resonant dog latin, may have struck
home among the Parisians of his day, but at the same time
they partake of the legendary life of the popular theater.
Molière found himself by perceiving afresh, and revivifying in
his own Paris, this legendary world, the comic picture of Man
in Society which the folk-theater of Latin Europe had been
making, off and on, for two thousand years—since Menander
the Greek.

It is even more important to remember that he learned
his wonderful mastery of the theatrical medium itself—the performer on the boards before an audience—from the Italian

improvisers. Molière's plays are conceived as *performances* before the words are written at all. His scenes could be mimed, or danced, or set to music; and they would be intelligible theatrically as music or dance or gymnastic clowning. *The School for Wives* contains some of the subtlest, wittiest language ever written for the stage; but beneath its rhymes and its verbal play there are the rhythms of slapstick: the mock duel, the beating, the chase, the skillful parry. Beneath the spiritual agility of an Arnolphe or Alceste there is the visible gymnastic agility of the comedian, actor and dancer in one, who improvises his laughable stratagems before an audience which sees, laughs, and understands at once.

It is this farcical basis of Molière's great comedy which seems so fresh and wonderful to us, but his contemporaries and his successors seem to have taken that for granted. What interested them was Molière's ideas, language, and contemporary social satire. Hence the notion of Molière as the Classic Author and the satirist of French manners, the counterpart in comedy of Racine and Corneille in tragedy. And one must remember that Molière did share the literary culture of French Classicism. If he could build the scenarios of the Commedia into literary works, it is partly due to his early education in Terence and Plautus, from whose plays the Commedia's scenarios were derived. If he could live up to the rationality, verbal elegance, and refinement of feeling of neoclassic literary taste; if he could reflect the types, language, and manners of the salons, it is because he had begun to acquire some of the literary culture early. He had, for instance, acted Corneille's tragedy when he first formed an acting company. A hundred years after Molière, Goldoni, in Venice, wishing to reform Italian comedy, proposed to emulate this development of Molière's toward contemporary satire and literary sophistication, by writing realistic character parts for the actors who were still playing the traditional masks of the Commedia: "Yes," he said to himself, "you must handle character subjects, they being the source of all good comedy. This is what Molière did, thus developing his art to a degree which the ancients only indicated, and which the moderns have not yet equalled."

Goldoni is only one of many writers of comedy all over Europe, in the seventeenth and eighteenth centuries, who followed Molière. And they all followed him in the same direction: away from the folk tradition of farce, and toward rationality, literature, and the realistic imitation of contemporary characters; in short, toward modern drama as we know it. If you remove from Molière's theater the legendary scope of the traditional masks of farce, and the peculiar mastery of the performer's art which goes with it, the way is clear for the thesis plays, the talky and sedentary parlor comedies, the well-made entertainments of our commercial theater. Molière is the father of the great form of neoclassic comedy, which lighted the theaters of Europe for a hundred and fifty years; and by the same token he is the grandfather of the modern theater. When one reads Molière now, one can still see the various aspects of his art which different generations have appreciated, and used for their purposes. These perspectives help one to come to know Molière. But his art is his own, and his comic genius, for all its clarity and universality, is unique.

Fortunately the cult of Molière's own plays has never died out. He is performed wherever the culture of Europe has spread, but especially, of course, in France. After his death his company was fused with that of the Hôtel de Bourgogne to make the Comédie Française. That most brilliant of state theaters, the "House of Molière" as it is often called, has survived all of the terrible vicissitudes of its native France. It flourishes still, with a more tenacious life than any other institution except the Church, or (as Henry James suggested) Parliament. James saw Molière performed there in 1872, and reported as follows: "Molière is played at the Théâtre Français as he deserves to be—one can hardly say more—with the most ungrudging breadth, exuberance, and *entrain,* and yet with a kind of academic harmony and solemnity. Molière, if he ever drops a kindly glance on MM. Got and Coquelin, must be the happiest of immortals. To be read two hundred years after your death is something; but to be acted is better." Thus Molière's own comedy plays still, a continuing source of the lore and the arts of the theater, and also, as Henry James put it, a "school of manners": for Molière is one of those great artists with the power to form the spirit which we call humane.

MOLIÈRE'S MAJOR PLAYS

Molière's most characteristic work extends from pure farce at one extreme to the most serious high comedy, in verse, at the other.

The Physician in Spite of Himself was written rather late in Molière's short career, in 1666, but it is a good example of the theatrical art which he learned from the Commedia, and which, as I have suggested, underlies all his work. It is based upon the Commedia's ancient comic themes: the old man with a troublesome daughter; the lusty and gymnastic clown; the sinister nonsense of the Doctor of Bologna. The reader should imagine it played with the lightness of the trapeze artist, in costumes suggesting the timeless masks of Pantalone, Zani, and the Doctor of Bologna.

The Highbrow Ladies and *The Miser* are among the plays in which the contemporary satire is most clear. *The Highbrow Ladies,* wonderfully good-natured, full of the honey and sunshine of Molière's youth, was certainly inspired by the highbrow Hôtel de Rambouillet. *The Miser,* a play of his maturity, is harder, and has a wider theme: the nonsense to which avarice reduces a whole family. The miser himself reincarnates the penny-pinching graybeards of the classical tradition of farce, but he is also a *bourgeois de Paris,* perhaps akin to Molière's own father.

The comedies of this type piqued the Parisians with their contemporary satire, but pleased them, perhaps, because of their clarity, rationality, and literary urbanity. In them one may understand Molière as one of those who formed the style of the period; a style, or taste, in which reason, in several senses, is so important a criterion: in Descartes' geometric method; in Racine's absolute and crystalline tragedy; in the symmetrical architecture and the rigidity of official manners. Molière's use of reason is singularly free for his age, because it is based upon common sense. In the light of common sense Molière's ideal *honnêtes gens* can see at once that his literary ladies, and his avaricious old man, are absurd: their ways of life are based upon glaringly false, and therefore laughable, premises. But upon these false premises they pursue their careers with the most perfectly logical consistency, until the inevitable débâcle, the practical *reductio ad absurdum* which even they must face. The texture of these comedies is rational: logical exposition and nimble dialectic. At the same time they are joyful celebrations of the absurdity to which rationalizing itself is pushed.

The Misanthrope, Tartuffe, and *The School for Wives* were written in verse, rhymed couplets with twelve syllables to the line, the famous *Alexandrines* in which Corneille and Racine wrote their tragedies. They are all high, or serious, comedy, and some have even said that they were tragic. It would be foolish to argue about the terms "comedy" and "tragedy" in this case; one certainly would not wish to say that Molière's comic vision did not have the depth usually attributed to tragedy. And yet one is likely to miss their peculiar greatness unless one sees that, whatever their implications, these plays are all, in their immediate effect, comedy.

The Misanthrope has been called a self-portrait, Molière's *Hamlet.* The comparison reveals something; and yet, as one reads the play, one must think of it as played, with energy and exactitude, before a laughing house. This point is well explained by Coquelin, the great French actor, in his study of the play published in 1881.* He says that to make Alceste a tragic character, a Hamlet, a Faust, a Jansenist, or Molière himself, would be a mere sentimental literary theory which would miss the values of the play on stage: an interpretation more in accord with nineteenth-century taste than with Molière's own practice. Molière could have understood misanthropy from his own experience, but he does not make Alceste the mouthpiece for his own philosophy. On the contrary, he presents him as the "atrabilious lover," irrationally but unmistakably caught by his love for Célimène, and therefore subject to the requirements of human intercourse as we all know them. In this tight and revealing situation he is funny, for all the depth of his hatred for the wordly game. The humor is very deep; but it is the greatness of the play that it keeps the perspective of comedy.

Behind *Tartuffe* you may, if you like, feel the chill of treachery itself. But that would come later, with after-thoughts. While the comedy is played on stage, Tartuffe's falseness looks like impudence and paradox: an impossibility, a farce, for the sane audience which sees and enjoys it. And Tartuffe's impudence, like Madame Pernelle's peevishness and Orgon's blind infatuation, is fed by Molière's own love for shameless human energy in all its forms.

The School for Wives is less likely than the other two to be mistaken for a tragedy in disguise, but it is certainly a play of equal depth. Behind Arnolphe's desperate efforts to confine Agnès's love within the rules of reason, one feels Molière's deli-

* Benoit Coquelin, *Molière et Le Misanthrope* (Paris: Ollendorff, 1881).

cate sense of the mystery of love itself. This comedy has all
its worldly wits about it. Molière himself never surpassed the
lightness and formal beauty of its dialogue: arabesques of
thought and feeling, the perfection of comic play. All this is in
the foreground; but behind or beneath the wit there is a
douceur akin to Shakespeare's tenderness, or to the modest
sweetness of seventeenth-century music.

The Theater of Paul Valéry

Valéry was the most self-conscious of artists. The creative or form-making power of the mind, the *virtu formativa*, was his central theme all his life. Much of his critical and philosophical prose is devoted to it, from "The Method of Leonardo" onward. Even his poems may often be read as poems about poem-making. He does not abandon this theme, or his habit of watching himself in the act of composition, when he writes for the theater. In the light of his other work and of his immediate comments his plays and librettos are clear: they are just what he intended them to be; they have a classic solidity and finality. For anyone who easily accepts Valéry—his intense and single theme, his extremely refined modes of thought—the theater pieces need little explanation or comment.

But for readers of English brought up in another tradition and another generation his whole work may look extreme and arbitrary. Eliot has written that Valéry will "remain for posterity the representative poet, the symbol of the poet, of the first half of the twentieth century—not Yeats, not Rilke, not anyone else." Valéry has, I suppose, carried certain aims of modern poetry to their logical conclusion. But Yeats, Rilke, Eliot himself, and many others have found un-Valerian sources and aims for their poetry. And if that is true of lyric poets it is even more true of poets of the theater. The theater poetry

of Lorca, like that of Chekhov, speaks in many voices, emerges
from a rich human context which is felt as real and significant.
Valéry on the contrary will have as little as possible to do
with the human situation in this guileless sense. He aims at
complete detachment, the absolute freedom of the mind in its
creativity, which in his radical view would mean freedom from
any object whatever except the form-making mind itself. His
famous formula for the completely self-conscious mind—*un refus
indéfini d'être quoi que ce soit*—means a rejection of other individuals also, their common world, and their relationships.
It may seem paradoxical therefore that he should wish to write
for the theater, that impure medium which is so deeply im-
mersed in the concreteness and variety of human life, so close
a reflection, in the hands of its masters, of the world of common experience.

It is this paradox which a reader in our time and place
must try to explore. What does the master of pure poetry propose to do with the impure medium of the theater? How does
Valéry, whose deepest aim is the ultimate abstraction, come to
terms with the stubborn concreteness of stage, audience, and
performers?

He does so in various ways, for he was led to write for the
theater at different times and for several different reasons. In
the fragments entitled *Mon Faust* it is the theme of Faust which
inspires him, and the dramatic form in which they appear is
accidental. The librettos on the other hand are occasional
pieces written for particular composers or performers, and in
writing them Valéry was trying primarily to make entertainments which would actually work in the theater.

II

The legend of Amphion, who first received the lyre from
Apollo, and through the formative power of music became the

father of the arts, inspired Valéry in his youth with its operatic possibilities, as he explains in his illuminating lecture on the libretto he finally wrote. The legend seemed to be the perfect illustration of the young Valéry's own theories of the creative process. Music, the most abstract of the arts, would be the closest to the *virtu formativa* itself, the freest from all entanglement with particular things. Next would come architecture with its nonrepresentational forms, the most abstract of the visual arts. Amphion, when he gets the lyre, produces music first, and then by its power enchants the savage scene (the world before the arts) to compose itself into forms for the eye: temples, terraces, and the like. Valéry originally planned the work as the "perfect opera," in which every detail on-stage, setting, movement, color, would strictly obey the music: a "despotic ideal," as Baudelaire said of Wagner's kind of opera. Valéry was probably directly influenced by Wagner's own notion of the *Gesamtkunstwerk*, by Nietzsche's Wagnerian theory of the birth of the arts from the spirit of music, and perhaps by Appia's plans for the staging of Wagner's operas. This youthful scheme was abandoned, but I think it shows what Valéry's basic feeling for the theater is. If he had committed himself seriously to the theater he would probably have tried to develop such a theatrical form as this: a form of despotic unity; a kind of musical theater analogous to the "pure" poetry of his lyrics.

But as he explains in his lecture, he got no encouragement for his first Amphion project when he asked Debussy to write the music for it. He abandoned Amphion for many years—until Honegger appeared—and then he wrote the present libretto. That work does not at first glance show the influence of the Wagnerian despotic ideal. It looks more like a neo-classic masque or *divertissement:* a treatment of the Greek legend in the rationalistic, Latin tradition, in which the legend is not religiously "believed" à la Wagner, but charmingly presented as an illustration of philosophic concepts. The bosky and rocky scene in which Amphion wakes and plays, the generalized human figures, the templed hills, own more to Poussin than to Appia. It looks like an urbane entertainment in a French style. But Valéry tells us that this *Amphion* embodies a "bizarre conception born of a theory-making mind"—and that conception represents another and more intellectual kind of despotic ideal; it bespeaks the authentic Valerian passion for pushing art to its theoretical limit. Pushed to the limit, as he says, *Amphion* in this version would approach liturgy. Liturgy has its abstractness too: it presents the generalized scenario of some mode or moment of human experience, and it is enacted by agents of little significance in themselves. The unindividualized figures in the pretty Greek tale are not themselves the substance of *Amphion*. Through them, as through a conventional sign language, we must read a "liturgical" enactment of the birth of the arts—if not a religious meaning, at least a scheme of final authority, a theoretic "limit" of human experience.

There is something paradoxical about inventing a liturgy, just as there is about inventing a myth. Perhaps that is why Valéry calls his conception "bizarre." The value of existing liturgies for their enviable believers is that they were not invented by a single mind, however deep and clear. Whatever their origins (in tradition, or the Word of God, or the subconscious), they are *given:* variously acceptable and understandable by many minds. Valéry's theoretic liturgy does not enjoy this advantage. It would not even be perceptible except to a highly select group capable of grasping his conventional use of the Greek legend, the authority of his theory of art, and the exciting paradox of his whole dramaturgic feat. Such an audience might find in *Amphion* (if the composer, designer, and performers were superbly good) a refined pleasure of the mind and of the senses.

III

Semiramis (1934) and *The Narcissus Cantata* (1938) were composed for the theater. Valéry's Preface to *Semiramis* explains his intentions in that work: he was dreaming, as usual, of a theater-poem in which all the elements would be strictly unified, as in a lyric; but he ruefully foresaw that the conceptions of collaborating performers, designers, and musicians would have to be taken into account. Like *Amphion*, it was set to music by Honegger. We also have the lyric poems, the *Air de Sémiramis* and the *Fragments du Narcisse*, on the themes of the librettos. The lyrics are certainly close to Valéry's own inspiration, and by comparing them with the librettos we may see what he did to meet the somewhat alien requirements of the stage.

The *Air de Sémiramis*, the song of the legendary savage queen as she dreams of absolute power, is an early work of Valéry's, but it has some of the musical beauty and allusive richness which we associate with his most famous poems. Absolute power is one phase, or face, of his notion of the mind's creative power. In the poem this theme is conveyed by the appropriate magic of the word, which creates the queen's terrible aspiration in the reader's imagination as the Word of God is supposed to have created the world. But in making the libretto Valéry was obliged to rely on the composer, the designer, and the performers to produce effects like those of the words and imagery of the poem. "The music should create an atmosphere of power and sovereign pride," he says; and he calls upon the designer to present to the physical eye the gigantic palace, the parapet in the morning light, and the smoking and swarming kingdom spread below. The poem has no narrative movement, but for the performers he provides a story: the queen's triumph over the neighboring kings; her lustful enjoyment of one of them; her rejection of lust in favor of murder, and her final ecstatic self-immolation in the rays of the morning sun.

Valéry was well aware of the difficulties his theatrical collaborators would face. In his discussion of *Amphion* he points out that Honegger's music must accomplish the paradoxical feat of leading the auditor musically from no music to music itself. All librettists must rely on their collaborators, but Valéry asks his to work at the edge of the theatric medium, and perhaps beyond it. The conception of *Semiramis* is clear, especially when compared with the poem; but to what extent is it realizable in the theater?

That depends of course on both audience and performers, and perhaps Valéry could ask the utmost of both. In his dialogue *Dance and the Soul* he describes a ballet with that combination of abstractness and richest allusiveness which we find in his verse. He believes that the inspired dancer might come as close as the musician himself to the invisible root of life. Perhaps he counted on such a dancer for *Semiramis*. But the role he wrote for her is not, like the ballet he describes, "pure" dance, corresponding to his own pure poetry, but a narrative sequence in which a human individual is all too scandalously visible. Could an audience, however accustomed to literary and theatrical conventions, watch the queen and her captive king wrestling among the cushions without a little unwanted laughter? It is when the concretely human shows through the conventional stage figure that Valéry's plan falters. The other side of his kind of intellectual rigor, the price of his theoretic strictness, is a kind of solemn and sensational crudity, which we feel whenever we are reminded of actual human relationships. In all his librettos there is a tension between the theoretic ideal and the perversity of the human image, which the public and all too human medium of the theater continually threatens to reveal. Choreographer and dancers would have to beware of this tension, treading with the utmost tact a tightrope course; and the written libretto does not give them much help with this problem: that of the *style* of the performance.

In *The Narcissus Cantata* this problem of style or convention is much less acute. It is the last of the librettos, the farthest from Valéry's deepest sources, and the easiest theatrically. Written at the request of Germaine Tailleferre, who composed the music, it is, as he says, quite different and quite distinct from the famous *Fragments du Narcisse.*

The *Fragments* constitute one of the triumphant versions of Valéry's own theme:

Que tu brilles enfin, terme pur de ma course!

Narcissus' contemplation of his own reflection in the pool is analogous to the end of philosophy as Dante describes it: "The philosophizing soul not only contemplates the truth, but also contemplates its own contemplation and the beauty thereof, turning upon itself and enamoring itself of itself by reason of the beauty of its direct contemplation." And this inward turn of love also suggests poetizing when it is so "pure" that poetry is taken as its own theme. Dante's formula is almost the "scenario" of the *Fragments du Narcisse.* For in those poems there is no narrative movement, no basic change, and no interplay between persons. The nymphs are dissolved in the evening air, the scene is dissolved in a harmony of echoes and reflections, all murmuring to Narcissus of his own beauty alone. But in the *Cantata* the whole conception has changed: we are no longer identified with Narcissus' enchanted solitude. The nymphs have their say, in their own voices, at the beginning, and when Narcissus gives his beautiful aria he is not alone. The situation produces a fight and dispute. The first nymph can tell Narcissus he has offended the gods:

Ton crime est d'ignorer tous les coeurs alentour.

Narcissus makes a choice; he rejects the will of the gods and the impure world with other people in it, in favor of purity which is perhaps nonentity.

Narcissus and the nymphs are more conventionalized figures than the characters in *Semiramis,* and the relation between them and human reality seems to be better understood and more frankly faced. The stage figures may represent human beings without danger to the whole conception, for the comic or perverse aspects of the story are accepted from the beginning. In planning the *Cantata* Valéry seems to have sacrificed his strictly lyric inspiration at the outset, and then worked within the theatrical conventions of the cantata and the neoclassic legend. He had great respect for conventions of all sorts: verse forms, musical or mathematical systems, and the like. The very arbitrariness of convention offered him an indispensable means for handling his favorite themes, in themselves so abstract that they had no necessary embodiment. By means of convention he can view his concrete material as coldly as he likes: as a mere sign of what transcends it. And in his account of the way he wrote *Le Cimetière marin* he tells us that his first inspiration for that poem was a certain stanzaic form. He felt his rhythms and harmonies abstractly before he got the "content" of the poem we know; if the conventional form was not the real root of the poem, it was at least what precipitated it. His acceptance of the cantata form and the conventional sign language of the legend seems to have precipitated *The Narcissus Cantata* in much the same way.

The librettos are not equally successful, but they are all, in intention at least, "poetry of the theater" as Cocteau defined it. One may understand this poetry by thinking over the sequence, not of words, but of the theatrically perceptible scenes and images as the librettos call for them. It is poetry akin to that of ballet, with a comparable economy and concentration, dependent like it upon a conventional vocabulary. But more than ballet it appeals also to the mind, reflecting as it does the author's brilliant and despairing spirit.

IV

In the prefatory note to *Mon Faust*, which Valéry addresses "to the wary but not unwilling reader," he gives us the clue to the proper reading. Goethe, he says, having taken Faust and Mephistopheles at the puppet stage, and by his genius raised them to the highest point of poetic existence, has made them available as instruments of the universal spirit: "He put them to the immortal purpose of expressing certain extremes of humanity and the inhuman; and in so doing he liberated them from any particular plot." Valéry proposes to place the two in our time ("dans notre espace") which is so different from Goethe's. It is, in short, the Faust theme at its highest level of abstraction which interests him. As for the plays themselves, he sketched them in quickly, he says, "with little care for plot, action, or ultimate scope." The use of the play form seems to have been chance, perhaps only an echo of Goethe's long conversation with himself.

The Faust theme offers a natural challenge to Valéry, especially as Goethe had handled it. What he says of Leonardo da Vinci applies to this Faust: "I regarded him as the principal character of that Intellectual Comedy which has still to find its poet and would, in my judgment, be far more precious than the *Comédie humaine;* more precious, even, than the *Divine Comedy.*" The comedy, the challenge, and the difficulty of the post-Goethian Faust is that when Faust is abstracted from the Christian framework of belief in which early versions had their being, it becomes impossible to define his form or meaning. Faust himself is regarded as a "limit," and so comes to mean or include everything—or nothing. Marlowe's Faust (whatever

Marlowe's own belief) had a real devil to sell his soul to, a
real soul, a real world to enjoy, and a real God to end his
story in damnation. But in Goethe's *Faust* all these elements
tend to lose their solidity. They fuse, change places, and begin
to "mean" each other, as they are digested into Faust's mind.
And if we then try to define or limit Faust himself, we are led
back to Goethe as he thinks over his experiences and the books
he has been reading. Though much has changed since Goethe,
as Valéry reminds us, the "comic" plight of Faust remains essentially the same; and the question is how a contemporary
author can reawaken the tired theme:

> Excite the membrane, when the sense has cooled,
> With pungent sauces, multiply variety
> In a wilderness of mirrors.

Thomas Mann felt the renewed pull of Faust at about the
same time as Valéry. He too is bitten by the appetite for the
limits of human experience, and he inhabits the same de-
humanized *espace* of contemporary intellectual Europe. But the
stratagems he employs in writing *Doctor Faustus* are the exact
opposite of those Valéry uses in *Mon Faust*. Mann makes a
massive frontal assault upon the Faust theme, to *prove* that it
is really the hidden machinery, the sinister fatality, of the whole
of contemporary culture. He is too serious and voluble to bother
with what used to be called "taste"; and though he flirts with
the reader, his purpose is not to charm, but to exhaust and
overpower him. Valéry, on the contrary, implies that he has
himself politely done the work in advance, and now presents
us with the result which we may take as lightly as we please:
a harmless-looking tube, in which (we are assured) absolute
vacuum has been approached as nearly as the most refined
modern methods for exhausting the air can do it; a sample of
the atmosphere at his and Faust's ultimate summit.

By settling for mere samples of Faustianism, Valéry eludes

Mann's unmanageable encyclopedism, and also his worst problems of form. But the basic difficulty, that of objectifying Faust dramatically, remains: if he has "read all the books," tasted and rejected all experience, and seen through all the arts and sciences, what (of any significance) can possibly happen to him? In *Luste, or The Crystal Girl,* Valéry leaves Faust in his motionless and invisible plight, but brings three more tangible characters into his orbit: Luste, his charming secretary, an agile version of the eternal feminine; a young disciple who seems bent on repeating the patterns of Faust's own distant youth; and Mephistopheles, now helpless and superannuated. It is these three who give the comedy its movement, and the audience its *frisson nouveau.*

We cannot tell how Valéry might have contrived an end to *Luste,* if he had been interested enough to finish it for the stage. It is perhaps *essentially* fragmentary in form, a sample of conversation: Valéry talking to himself "in two voices," as he puts it. But the genre of this sample is intellectual comedy akin to that of Shaw or Giraudoux, and Valéry masters its tone and movement with extraordinary ease. He weaves a texture which is both witty and delicately lyrical; perhaps the most promising and congenial theatrical vein he discovered.

The other fragment of *Mon Faust*—an apparently unrelated variation—seems to me much less successful. The Only One, on an empty mountaintop beyond the arctic life zone, an intellect which has accepted the ultimate rigor, the ultimate poverty, to the point where his sense of reality is expressed by a wolf's howl to the stars, has out-Fausted Faust. When Faust toils painfully up to his cold rock, having left poor old Mephistopheles behind long since, the Only One contemptuously tosses him over the cliff, down to the homier and more impure region where organic life may exist. So the contemporary Faust is defined—dramatically objectified—by the Only One, as the Christian God had demonstrated the limits of Marlowe's Faust.

The plan of this piece is intelligible enough; even too intelligible. But how is it to be taken? Valéry calls it *une féerie,* and it is nearer to the genre of the librettos than to any species of modern comedy. Even more than in the librettos the tension between its ambitious, even solemn, thought, and the characters and scenes which fill the stage itself, is disturbing.

Disturbing at least for one who (like an urchin in the ruins of Nineveh) is not really at ease with "The Crisis of the European Mind." Perhaps most of us who read Valéry's theater works on this side of the Atlantic, and in another generation, must feel that his "extremes of humanity and the inhuman" are somewhat alien to us when he spells them out for the stage. The great lyrics may be enjoyed as "pure" poetry, on the analogy of music: with little regard to their provenance or their concrete relevance. But in the theater pieces we are reminded, from time to time, that we have not read all the books, and that the "Mind" we know something about is suffering from malnutrition rather than the frustrations of omniscience. And then a difficult effort of sympathy is required if we are to see the effects Valéry intended, his ironic and suggestive play with the limits of his thought, at the limit of the theater medium.

Oedipus According to Freud, Sophocles, and Cocteau

NOTE: This paper was originally written for Dr. Leslie Farber, who was arranging a series of discussions at the Washington School of Psychiatry on the general topic of character, as it is represented in Freudian psychology on the one hand, and in literature or drama on the other.

The legendary Oedipus is I suppose the most obvious instance of a character who has been important both in drama and in Freudian theory, and that is why I have chosen him as a point where the relation between psychopathology and poetry in the widest sense may conveniently be considered. I wish to enquire first what understanding of Oedipus the man, the individual character, we may get from Freud—and I mean Freud's own classic writings. (I have the impression that modern theory is much more sophisticated than the early Freud, but it is Freud himself who exercises the wider influence.) I then wish to compare Freud's Oedipus with that of Sophocles, and then, by way of experimental control, with Cocteau's more up-to-date dramatization of the same ancient myth. I speak of Freud with great timidity, for I have no practical knowledge of psychoanalysis, never having been "psyched," and possessing only a layman's secondhand knowledge of the theory. My point of view is that of the non-technical enquirer who seeks, in all innocence, to get a little light on human character.

Such an enquirer is likely to find Freud's theory both startling and simple. He wrote in 1910: "The myth of King Oedipus, who kills his father and wins his mother as a wife, is *only* the slightly altered presentation of *the* infantile wish, rejected later by the opposing barriers of incest." (my italics) At that point in his thinking Freud regarded the famous Oedipus Complex—the hidden need of incest and murder—as the unseen but universal basis of human character. In *Totem and Taboo* he went on to present it as the actual prehistoric basis of all human society also. Laws, ethical codes, literatures, religions, appear in this theory as alterations or sublimations or disguises of the motives of the Oedipus complex, that "natural" set of drives which we are supposed to share with the great apes.

This glum scenario has proved very congenial to the modern mind, but, as I have suggested, it strikes me as too simple a picture of the psyche "in nature," that is, before civilization diverts it from its congenital aims. It takes no account, for example, of the creative or formative activity of the preconscious mind, which psychology in the Greek tradition regards as its essential nature, and which all scientists, artists, and thinkers rely on—as much as they rely on the efforts of their conscious minds—when they are engaged in a long piece of original work. The Oedipus Complex is also too simple, not to say simpleminded, when applied to the analysis of particular characters of history, poetry, or legend. Take, for example, Ernest Jones's book on Hamlet and Oedipus.* In order to prove that Shakespeare's play is only a thin disguise of Shakespeare's own Oedipus complex, he has to identify Shakespeare with Hamlet, forgetting that Shakespeare must also be identified with Polonius, Ophelia, the Gravedigger, and all the other characters in the play, all of whom he fed with his own feelings—and forgetting also the other great tragedies, and the joyful comedy

* Ernest Jones, *Hamlet and Oedipus* (New York, 1949).

of *Twelfth Night*, which Shakespeare wrote in the same period of a few years. But Jones does not mind psychoanalyzing Shakespeare and Hamlet at once, thereby reducing their characters, along with those of Sophocles and his King Oedipus, to the same mechanism; for that mechanism, that faceless need of murder and incest, strikes him as more real and more significant than the individuals who unconsciously harbor it. At this point the innocent enquirer is likely to feel that Freud has made "character" of all kinds disappear.

If one then re-reads Sophocles' play, *Oedipus Rex*, one is refreshed by finding a living, credible individual being, with all the concrete elements of temperament, of talent, of destiny, which real individuals must have.

First of all, Oedipus has a unique story, most of which did not interest Freud at all. He was warned by the oracles, when he was a boy, that he was fated to kill his father and wed his mother. To escape that fate, he leaves Corinth, for he erroneously believes that it is his real home, and the Corinthian King and Queen his real parents. By an extraordinary series of circumstances he does in fact kill an older man, who will turn out to be his real father, and weds the Queen of Thebes, his real mother. When Sophocles' play opens, Oedipus, as King of Thebes, is obliged to dig up the facts of the old murder, and to face them, one by one, as they reveal the terrible things he has done.

As Sophocles presents the story he does not seem to be suffering from the repressed desires of the Complex, nor does he suggest that his characters are. When Oedipus kills his father in a fit of temper, he can hardly have intended patricide, since he had not seen the old man since he was an infant only a few days old—though I admit that for Freud any tension between a young man and an older one springs from the Complex. When Oedipus tells Jocasta, his wife and mother, that he still fears the oracle, she remarks that many men dream of lying with their mothers. This notion has not been repressed by either her or her son: what bothers them is not suppressed desires, but what they may unwittingly have *done*. And what moves Oedipus and his audience is not an appetite for lust and violence, but an even more perilous need, that of the truth, cost what it may.

In order to make this story credible and moving as drama, Sophocles pictures Oedipus as an individual with many sides to his nature, a "character" in the old commonsense meaning of the term. Oedipus is a vigorous, intelligent man, noted also for the special insight he displayed when he solved the Sphinx's riddle. He is a responsible ruler, and as the crisis in Thebes and in his own affairs deepens he meets it with great moral courage, but at the same time with his temperamental pride, hastiness, or "hubris" as the Greeks called it. We come to know him as we know people in life; it is not hard to sympathize with him in his terrible struggle, and to share his dismay as the truth appears.

In this play the human setting is of fundamental importance in the portrayal of Oedipus, his motives, and his fate. Sophocles assumes the complex order of the Greek City-State, for that is the basis of Oedipus's role as King and father of his people. The traditional order of society and of family, which all the *dramatis personae* wish to preserve, would be destroyed by incest, or murder, or treason, or other crimes. It was supposed to be natural, and also divinely sanctioned; it was not hidden, represssed, or illusory, and the deeds that might imperil it were well and clearly known. It is not hard to see that a man who, like Oedipus, had unknowingly and fortuitously undermined his community, had thereby undermined his own being: his "character" as King, husband, son, and father depended upon the society that defined and recognized these functions.

Nowadays the word "Oedipus" means to us the Freudian

theory, not the tragedy in which Sophocles incarnated the ancient myth. But I think the non-technical enquirer could find more light on human character by reading *Oedipus Rex*, and meditating upon the many and diverse concrete elements of temperament, fate, and cultural tradition in Sophocles' portrait, than he could by uncritically accepting the theory that replaces it in the public mind.

So far we have been considering only Freud's theory, as expounded in his writings, for that is much more accessible to the layman than the practical lore of psychoanalysis. But I suppose that the analyst uses the theory only as a guide-line or preliminary hypothesis, when he engages in the work of therapy or research. And I should think that the most valuable Freudian lore of Character would emerge from the labors of the analysts with their patients. It is unfortunate that this lore can only reach us secondhand: in case histories, and in humorous, or sensational, or religiously solemn anecdotes of the famous couch. But the process of psychoanalysis, however inadequately understood, is now part of our general culture. Let us see how it looks to the unregenerate public, as a source of light on character.

When I first read a little Freud, about forty years ago, I was struck by a remark of the French critic, Ramon Fernandez. He said he thought Freud was having a beneficent influence on young people, because he presented the life of the youthful psyche in dynamic terms, as a struggle between various forces within the individual who, just emerged from childhood, had some hope of making (or choosing) himself. In contrast with the academic psychology that had prevailed in France, which tended to be static and rationalistic, Fernandez said, Freud recognized the importance of passion, conscious and unconscious, and the essentially changeable nature of the psyche's life.

This notion appealed to me, and it encouraged me to think

of the process of analysis as itself dynamic and changing—
dramatic, therefore, in a certain sense. When the analyst tries
to help a real individual in the real world, he must confront
something much more urgent, puzzling and unmanageable than
Freud's diagram: even more than the dramatist he is perforce
involved in the actualities of character. He must, I suppose,
try to deal with his patient's intelligence, insight, moral stamina,
and imagination, as well as his suppressed desires. He must
learn to know the characters who have played important parts
in the patient's story, and are important in his present situation.
Moreover in this tangled drama the doctor must play a part
himself, not only as the detached eye of scientific truth, or the
wielder of an infallible method, but as an individual who takes
sides in the therapeutic struggle. In that situation, I suppose,
a knowledge of human character derived from any source,
Freudian or not, would come in handy, as well as a wide
familiarity with the human jungle of modern society in which
the struggle for sanity must ultimately be decided. If this picture is not too wide of the mark, then Fernandez was right
in thinking of a psychoanalysis as dramatic. The analyst, as
he endeavors to guide his patient, would be dealing with many
of the same problems as the dramatist, who tries to control the
form and movement of his story. There would be analogies between the art of therapy (as distinguished from the abstract
Freudian theory) and the art of the dramatist, different though
their ostensible aims may be.

One may compare the plot of Sophocles' tragedy with the
course of an analysis—if I am right in thinking that the first
aim of the analyst is to lead his patient to recognize certain
unwelcome truths. At the beginning of Sophocles' tragedy, King
Oedipus finds himself in a crisis which disturbs him deeply,
and which he knows he does not fully understand. He feels
threatened in his status as King and father of his City, and

therefore in his whole conception of himself. To deal with this crisis he is obliged to uncover certain facts: facts, it soon appears, of his own past life. He starts with those which he does not find hard to recall as bare facts. He easily remembers that he killed an older man, with whom he got into a fight, at a place where three roads meet; that he reached Thebes soon thereafter, and met the Queen Jocasta. But under the pressure of the enquiry he returns to the facts again and again, and he begins to recover the actual scenes in their sensuous details and their emotional charge; and then, to his growing terror, he slowly recognizes the significance of the surrounding circumstances. He gets a succession of insights which imperil his whole conception of who and what he is; but at each painful illumination he makes a new rationalization that postpones his recognition of the reality. He is sustained in this whole process by the Chorus, who recognize him as he appears at each stage, and sanction his heroic motive of digging up the truth, perilous though it be. When it is finally present to his spirit—when he accepts it emotionally and even sensuously—the character he had thought he was is gone. He is neither the King, nor the father, nor the husband, nor the son he had thought himself, but something hitherto unseen, and very scary. The play ends at that point, which corresponds, I think to the moment when the patient, with the aid of the analyst, has dug up repressed material. The analyst would then presumably go on to put his patient together again on a sounder foundation, and Sophocles, in his last play *Oedipus at Colonus*, went on to portray Oedipus as he became at last: the fierce old blind man whose inner vision made him a kind of natural saint, like his counterpart, the blind seer Tiresias.

So much for the parallels between the plot of tragedy and the plot of psychoanalysis that I am positing. But the differences between the two are as significant as their similarities.

I have already pointed out that Sophocles' characters do not seem to suffer from repressed desires to murder their fathers and sleep with their mothers, as Freud believed that all of his patients did. What Oedipus and Jocasta find it hard to face is not their desires, but the knowledge of what they have actually done. It is hard for them to accept that knowledge, because what they did in apalling blindness undermined their lives and the lives of their children, and imperiled the health of the whole patriarchal community. Their terror is not that of incestuous or patricidal passion, but the far wider terror of what we may do unwittingly. The combination of unwilled and unknown patricide and incest owes its effectiveness in the play of Sophocles, not to its attractiveness but to its destructiveness. Dryden in his version of *Oedipus* was rather fascinated with incest itself, but Sophocles uses it simply as an all-purpose booby-trap, the perfect device for mocking man's pretension to conscious control of his destiny. "Don't presume to say how happy a man is until his life has all been unrolled," as the Chorus remarks at the end.

Of course *Oedipus Rex*, being a Greek tragedy, was played in public, for many people simultaneously, and in this respect is very different from the *tête-à-tête* of the famous couch. Oedipus, though so deeply shaken, is not really insane, and the audience, though presumably in need of purgation, would hardly think of itself as pathological in our modern sense. The performance is an integral part of the seasonal Festival of Dionysos, an institution with religious, social, and familial meanings. The drama is, moreover, intended to provide the pleasures of harmony, like music, or any other art. Freud, when he recognizes art, likes to describe it as fantasy, a pleasant and nonpathological disguise of the author's suppressed desires. But Aristotle, a more sober and sophisticated observer, included "recognition" among the satisfactions offered by tragedy, for he thought it embodied, together with its harmonies, a kind of perception of truth, which the audience liked to confirm as it watched the play.

Aristotle also thought (as everyone knows) that a successful tragedy "purged" the audience through a combination of pity and fear, and the purgative effect of tragedy is another analogy with psychoanalysis. I have already suggested that the Chorus in *Oedipus Rex* assists Oedipus to recognize the truth, as the physician is supposed to do with his patient. The Chorus also shares, by sympathy, in Oedipus's fears and sufferings, as his being is painfully opened up to a wider awareness, and the audience reacts as the Chorus does, its own emotions stirred as the protagonist's are. But in order to get this effect the audience would not have to catch itself in the act of lusting after its mothers and yearning to murder its fathers; it would merely need to sense the terror of the unknown parts of its own being and destiny, and identify itself, in pity, for the moment at least, with Oedipus's plight. The whole process is much easier because it is common to many people, there in the thronged theater; many who simultaneously "recognize" some general truth of the human situation, and so become a bit quieter and wiser than they were.

So much for a very sketchy account of the similarities and differences between Freud's and Sophocles' Oedipus. This theme might be developed indefinitely, if one had the requisite knowledge, for Sophocles' treatment of the ancient myth has been more or less instructively interpreted for two thousand years, and the lore of the Oedipus Complex accounts for an impressive part of our contemporary conception of human character. But Sophocles' great play comes to us from the vanished world of fifth-century Athens, and his city and his theater provided him with resources for understanding and representing human character which the modern playwright lacks. That is why I wish, before I conclude, to talk a little about Cocteau's play, *The Infernal Machine*, which emerges from our own Freudian world.

Cocteau should cast a different light on our topic: character as it interests a dramatist, and character as Freud teaches us to conceive it.

The Infernal Machine has four acts, of which the last covers the same crisis as Sophocles shows in his whole play, and this act is based closely on Sophocles' plot. The first three acts are Cocteau's own, and in them one can see how a very gifted and sophisticated modern dramatist takes account of Freudian ideas in order to make his characters acceptable to a contemporary audience. These first three acts present episodes from the earlier lives of Oedipus and Jocasta, leading up to the moment when their tragic destiny overtakes them.

The first act is chiefly a portrait of Jocasta, as she was just before Oedipus came to Thebes and solved the riddle of the Sphinx. She is a youngish widow, spoiled and neurotic, troubled by a longing for a young man like her lost son—as she almost suspects herself. She reveals her partially-repressed desires in the dreams she reports, in her interest in a young soldier, and in many small accidents and slips of the tongue.

The second act, which is supposed to occur at the same time as the first, is centered on the young Oedipus as he meets the Sphinx on his way to Thebes. He is a shrewd, brash, and ambitious youth, rather inhibited sexually. We learn that he has little erotic interest in girls, but has always dreamed of being loved by an older woman. He doesn't repress any of this: he knows just what his tastes in sex are, but they don't strike him as a problem; he is chiefly interested in success of the most routine variety. He wants to win fame, fortune, and power, and, at last, to marry the boss's daughter.

The third act presents the wedding night. The bedroom is red, like the interior of a butcher-shop or a womb, and it contains a crib and a bed with a cover made of an animal's hairy hide. Oedipus and Jocasta, wearied by the long royal wedding ceremonies, move sleepily toward this bed. They are trying to tell each other little lies about their past lives, but in their somnolent state they continually get dreamlike associations with both the crib and the bed, and we feel that they can almost, but not quite, realize that they are mother and son.

It is evident that these three acts owe much more to Freud than they do to Sophocles. The lies, dreams, and slips of the tongue that plague Oedipus and Jocasta might have come straight out of Freud's *Psychopathology of Everyday Life*. The young Oedipus and the neurotic aging Jocasta seem to have been designed by Cocteau in order to be understood according to Freud's favorite complex. The choral voice that serves to introduce the play credits the gods with the machinery of fate, or chance, that brings Oedipus and Jocasta together, but in these first three acts Cocteau invites his sophisticated audience to think that it is the Freudian appetite for incest that more inevitably seals their doom. The red and hairy bedroom makes Freud's Oedipal situation obviously—even too obviously—present to the imagination.

Cocteau, of course, intends this emphasis upon the hidden machinery, Freudian or fatal; and in the first three acts Oedipus and Jocasta are not to be taken as full human characters. When Cocteau wrote this play, interest in human character, and in careful elaborate individual portraiture, such as we find in nineteenth-century fiction and in the plays of Ibsen and Chekhov, was on the wane. He does not ask us to take Oedipus and Jocasta very seriously, but to recognize them at a glance as we do the types on the society page or in parlor comedy: trivial and easily-spotted clichés of modern urban life. But all the while they are on the verge of seeing the sinister machinery, and this near-awareness gives these three acts a poetic dimension which parlor comedy lacks. It also carries us on to Act IV, in which Cocteau, after such careful preparation, endeavors to reaffirm the Sophoclean theme.

In the last act Oedipus faces one by one the facts that

reveal what he has done. He takes them with the stony face of the losing gambler, until the end, when Jocasta kills herself, and then, broken at last, he puts out his eyes. The blind Oedipus, his dead mother-wife Jocasta, and his daughter-sister Antigone move off the stage in a ghostly procession into the indefinite future. We are supposed to feel that Cocteau as author has made the ancient theme live again, by showing us Oedipus, Jocasta, and Antigone with the inhuman beauty and immortality of figures of legend. All of this works, I think, very well in the theater.

But to return, once more, to the portrayal of character, which is so different in the last act from what it was in the first three. Tiresias, the blind seer, is on hand to explain the change in the tone of the play here at the end. He says that the cruel machine of the gods has transformed Oedipus from a "playing-card king" into a man. In orthodox Freudian terms one would say, I suppose, that Oedipus had recognized his infantile wishes, and so grown up at last. From the point of view of Cocteau's work as dramatist, one might say that he had led his audience from a Freudian-psychopathological to a Sophoclean-humane view of the meaning of the Oedipus myth.

Cocteau's view of character in this play is akin to Freud's, not only because he owes so much directly to Freud's ideas, but because he lived in the same modern world, where many of the insights and beliefs that used to guide the poets are lost or discredited. But in one very important respect he differs from Freud: he can still see Sophocles' version of the ancient myth as significant. When Freud read the play he seems to have seen it merely as a pleasant and harmless disguise of the myth, which, in turn, was for him "only the slightly altered presentation of the infantile wish," that is, of his favorite complex. It did not occur to him to study the play itself as a source of valid insights. But that is just what Cocteau endeavors to do. He reaffirms both the unique life, and the perennial and very general fertility of the ancient tragedy. He tries to make us see it again as a celebration of human nature in its mysterious and perilous situation. He invites us to meditate on the vision it embodies as a means toward understanding our own situation.

Ibsen's *The Lady From the Sea*

The play I have chosen to write about—*The Lady from the Sea*—is not usually supposed to be one of Ibsen's best. But I have two reasons for wishing to introduce it into our discussions. The first is that I staged it, years ago, at Bennington College, and in working on it for three or four months I grew to know it, and to love and admire it. The second and more important reason is that Ellida's cure, or "change of heart" as one might call it, is almost unique in the plays of Ibsen's maturity. I think *Little Eyolf* is the only other one in which the protagonists learn to understand and transcend their disastrous motives. *The Lady from the Sea* has, therefore, a very special light to shed on the meaning of Ibsen's tragic vision of man in the modern *saeculum*.

In working on the play at Bennington we came to see that it is beautifully composed in every detail, so as to embody a single action, or motive, as Aristotle said any good drama must be. All of the characters we meet in Dr. Wangel's household feel that they are missing out; that they are somehow separated from the life and the love they need and cannot find; and the motive they all share in their different ways is to end that separation before it is too late. Ellida, with her longing for the far-off sea and the dimly-remembered Stranger is the most striking and desperate embodiment of this lost and nostalgic motive. But both of her stepdaughters, Boletta and Hilda, are moved in analogous ways. That is partly because they are in the transition period of youth, when everyone fears that he's missing life; partly because Ellida quite unintentionally makes everyone around her feel lonely and lost. The men all wish to "join the ladies," so to speak. Dr. Wangel wants to reach Ellida, who, he fears, is slipping farther and farther away from him; Arnholm, Boletta's old tutor, wishes to reach *her*, and the young sculptor Lyngstrand, who is dying of tuberculosis, wants to day-dream about pretty ladies day-dreaming about him. Even Ballested, the happy handyman and amateur painter, shares the prevailing vague, romantic impulse to escape, but he has long since come to terms with it. "One can learn to become acclimatized," he keeps telling the others: "acclimatized" here, in this rather dead and empty little town; acclimatized in the real world, which is less "thrilling," as Hilda would say, than day-dreams fed with frustration. When all the characters have taken Ballested's advice and become acclimatized, the action of the play is over.

As usual, Ibsen uses his setting, the season, and the times of day to make the audience share the underlying motive, as a lyric poet uses metaphor. The Doctor's pleasant house and garden command a view of the fjord leading out to the open sea; and one can watch the excursion steamer coming in from the ocean and the great world, and then departing again, with its distant band-music. The season is summer, but late summer, which must soon give place to the dark and lonely winter. In the first act, a prologue, we see the garden, the house, and the view, but in subsequent acts Ibsen uses different aspects of his basic setting to bring out the successive stages of the action. For the second act he places us on a height where we can look far out toward the sea, illuminates it with evening light, and accompanies it with distant sounds of voices and music, in order to prepare for Ellida's gloomy passion even before she presents it to poor Wangel in her prose lyric about the gulls, the whales, and the strange-colored eyes of her sailor-lover. Ibsen places the third act in a dark, enclosed part of the garden, with only a glimpse of the fjord visible between tall mountains; and there Hilda and the doomed boy Lyngstrand are stalking the huge old carp in the silent pond. It is a spot where strange forms of life might be expected to appear, if we proceed stealthily. And when Ellida wanders in, in a state of vague excitement, both prey and huntress, the Stranger himself soon makes his enigmatic appearance behind the little fence.

It used to be the fashion to describe such elements as the pond and the open sea, the carp and the freer ocean fishes, as "symbols." But I think we are all tired of hearing about Ibsen's symbolism, as though it were a unique and heavy-handed device peculiar to *his* art. Professor John Northam has done us a great service in enabling us to understand this matter in other ways. In his excellent book on Ibsen's technique he has pointed out that *all* of the visual, or other sensuous elements in Ibsen's plays, are essential and very consciously employed parts of his theater-poetry. Not only the obvious "symbols," but everything we see and hear, including the characters, has symbolic value, both for the *dramatis personae* and for the audience. That is because the human psyche lives primarily in a visible and audible world, and it is only by what we see and hear that we come to some knowledge of each other's inner lives, or express our own deepest needs. In his awareness of this fact, and in his realistic use of it to represent the life of the spirit, Ibsen was not only a nineteenth-century Symbolist, but a dramatic poet in the central tradition. As Dante wrote when preparing for *The Divine Comedy*, in which the life of the spirit is made sensuously-perceptible in so many ways, "the inner quality of the soul may be recognized by examing outwardly the things which it loves."

In working on *The Lady from the Sea* in order to make

as faithful a performance as possible, one discovers richer and richer patterns in it, as I have said. But I must admit that our audiences didn't quite share my enthusiasm. No doubt they would have liked the play better if the production had been better. But as I watched their reactions I thought I could understand why so many of Ibsen's admirers find it the least satisfying of the plays of his maturity.

Henry James called *The Lady from the Sea,* in an article written in 1891, "much the weakest, to my sense, of the whole series." James thought that the style, or attitude, that Ibsen adopted in this play, was wrong for the theme:

> The idea might have sprung from the fancy of Hawthorne, but the atmosphere is the hard light of Ibsen. One feels that the subject should have been tinted and distanced; but, in fact, one has to make an atmosphere as one reads, and one winces considerably under "Doctor Wangel" and the pert daughters.

For James, "Doctor Wangel" connotes, he says, "the ugly interior," and "the pervasive air of small interests and standards, the sign of limited local life." I think James may have missed the effect of Ibsen's carefully contrived settings, which is precisely to place, and thereby transcend, the "limited local life." And I think that if the play were properly acted the performance itself would "distance" and "tint" it. Perhaps that's what James means by "making the atmosphere as one reads": Ibsen, like other pure dramatists, must be read with full histrionic make-believe, if one is to get the intended effect of the play.

My experience with actual performances suggests, however, that James was right about the "pert daughters," especially Boletta and her prosaic middle-aged suitor Arnholm. The progress of their affair is hardly worth the clear, sober light, and the long stage-time, that Ibsen devotes to it. In the proposal scene in the fifth act, for instance, we know at once that Arnholm wants to marry Boletta, though that green and self-absorbed girl does not; and we tire of their scene long before it reaches its foregone conclusion. Chekhov, ten years later, was to learn how to bring out the humor and pathos in even the most clumsy and commonplace love affairs—by presenting them very briefly, and without asking the audience to take their outcomes too seriously.

The comparison with Chekhov is, I think, not inappropriate, for *The Lady from the Sea* anticipates Chekhov more than any of Ibsen's other plays. The theme of provincial nostalgia is Chekhovian, and so is much of the art, which relies, to an unusual extent for Ibsen, on ensemble moods and rhythms, and upon setting, lighting, and carefully-timed sound-effects. But, of course, Ellida's struggle, which came to absorb Ibsen's interest, is not Chekhovian at all, but an Ibsenesque "drama of ethical motivation." Ellida and her "cure" is the chief *raison d'être* of the play, and of these remarks.

Ellida is, first of all, a woman, one of those great women of Ibsen's who, different as they are from each other, all fail to find satisfaction in the common life around them. I am thinking, of course, of Nora, Hedda, Rebecca West, Mrs. Alving. Ibsen must have embodied much of his own discontent, scorn for the narrow bourgeois scene, and passionate aspiration toward the new and the unknown, in these figures. But he made each one of them a completely objectified individual in her own right: a woman, with a woman's place in society and a woman's destiny. Ellida, like the others, must be seen first as a woman. If she produces such deep and ambivalent feelings in Boletta and Hilda, it is because they identify themselves with her; they love and envy her as a woman. Not that they understand her trouble; they simply respond instinctively to what she feels and does. The men around Ellida respond to her also, of course; her emotion attracts their emotion. Ellida is like a great prima donna of the dramatic or operatic stage: a creature designed by nature as a sadly beautiful image of everyone's ineffable pathos. She is the role which every authentic tragic actress must dream of; no wonder the great Duse found her particularly congenial.

The spirit that possesses Ellida is, I think, very much like the one we know in many of Ibsen's male heroes also. Brand and Peer Gynt show two contrasting faces of it, and then come the more naturalistic portraits of Gregers Werle with his relentless ideal, the "integrity fever" as Dr. Rolling calls it; old Ekdal with his wild duck; Solness, Rubek, and Lövborg, with their perilous and creative inspirations. This spirit is usually presented in the imagery of the empty, alluring and frightening northern wilderness: high mountain country, or the cold ocean with its whales and its gulls, like the one Ellida dreams of. It is often felt as an objectively real demon that takes possession of the gifted man or woman, and pushes him to creative or destructive action. Is there any way to hypostatize this spirit, or to define it accurately? I doubt it. The late Paul Elmer More pointed out that the literature of the last century is full of it, "the Demon of the Absolute" as he called it; but he didn't succeed in making a very satisfactory description of it. Thomas Mann in *Dr. Faustus,* and Paul Valéry in *Mon Faust,* made very sophisticated studies of its nature and its habits. But it is a protean demon, as Peer Gynt discovered quite early; it is its very essence to elude moral philosophy, and it refuses to be embodied in a single *dramatis persona.* This spirit, this restless demon, is of course not completely embodied in Ellida; she is a different woman from Rebecca or Nora, and in her the spirit of rejection and undefined aspiration takes its own appropriate form. But in this play Ibsen is more than usually committed to the effort of seeing it clearly, defining it and controlling it. He invites the audience to understand Ellida by analogy with Boletta and Hilda; and at the same time he wants us to follow the Doctor as he isolates his wife's obsession, and at last dispels it, as though it were a disease, like young Werle's "integrity fever."

Thus Boletta finds her whole life in Dr. Wangel's household stultifying, like that of the carp, with their low but stubborn vitality; and all that she says on this theme applies to Ellida. When Arnholm tries humbly to court her, she finds him good, but can't recognize her romantic day-dreams in him. Ellida's feeling about Dr. Wangel is very much like Boletta's about Arnholm—blind and selfish—though she has the grace to try to apologize for it. Hilda also, like her sister and stepmother, feels that she is missing life here in Dr. Wangel's household; and in her case she feels that she is left out of even what little life the others have. She is more imaginative and intense than Boletta; she has a childish version of Ellida's rather deathly desperation. Lyngstrand brings out various analogies between the three women. Ellida is his inspiration for the romantic-sinister sculptured group he dreams about; he wants the more domesticated Boletta to dream about *him* as he sculpts in Rome; and Hilda he accepts as a playmate, not understanding that it is his approaching death that feeds *her* day-dreams. Lyngstrand serves to keep the notion of death before us, just as Dr. Rank does in *A Doll's House*. The sense of death, whether as romantic pose, Freudian "death wish," or too-close end, seems to be an indispensable ingredient in the recipe for the spirit that has Ellida in its grip. Thus the minor characters help us to understand Ellida by analogy; but it is primarily the Doctor who shows us Ellida's disease, as he tries to diagnose it. The Doctor is neither tempted nor made desperate by death, like the women in his house: he wants to save, or restore, their life together; and so he endeavors to "cure" the spirit that separates them, and that pulls Ellida, especially, away from him. As he approaches the truth, he has to face more and more painful facts, and sacrifice more and more of what he had thought of as his own life. As he gradually realizes that Ellida and his daughters are estranged, and then that Ellida can't really live here, he is ready to give up the home and the professional life he had built up. When at last he sees that his power and authority as a man and a husband (which could destroy the Stranger) would not avail to save Ellida, he relinquishes that too. In this struggle, both the nature of Ellida's disease, and its cure, are brought to light; the "cure" is experimental proof that the diagnosis, so painfully arrived at, was correct.

Some years ago when I was studying *Ghosts* I was struck by the similarity between Ibsen's picture of Mrs. Alving and Dante's picture of Ulysses in the twenty-sixth canto of the *Inferno*. Not only Mrs. Alving, but Nora, Rebecca, and creative men like Lövborg, Solness, and Rubek have the same imperious and impatient need that Ulysses expresses: to acquire virtue, knowledge, and experience of the unexplored world— at once, before the inevitable coming of death makes it all too late. Dante not only portrays this irresistable appetite, or aspiration; he shows its place in human experience. It is good in itself, it may even be called the basic motivation of the rational human psyche; but when unenlightened it leads to disaster. Ulysses is wrapped in the flame of the admirable appetite within him; he can see neither the love of his wife, his son, and his father, nor the limitations of the human condition. It is a milder form of this natural appetite for life and fulfillment that possesses Ellida and the two girls. In them, as in Ulysses, it is good and natural, but potentially lethal because they can see nothing outside the appetite itself.

Ellida's passion is similar not only to Ulysses', but also to other passions of Hell, notably Paolo's and Francesca's: it is tyrannical, permitting nothing outside itself. But the Doctor's is "the passion that purges;" the kind we see, in a light both classical and Christian, in Dante's ascent of the Purgatorial

Mountain. Driven by his love for Ellida and his daughters, the Doctor suffers, in several stages, the painful truths of his own helplessness and Ellida's imprisonment in her blind obsession. He is rewarded with clearer understanding, and at last with Ellida's change of heart, or "conversion," as it used to be called. Ellida's change, or cure, seems to be due both to what the Doctor can show her, and to what he has given her: he has, in some sense, suffered *for* her. The miraculous cure is "proved" when Ellida herself realizes that her cherished "freedom," which the Doctor gives her at great cost to himself, does not really consist in following her unregenerate passion, as she had assumed, but in the power to choose her own course, according to her new, clarified vision of herself, of other people, and of the real world. The Doctor has freed both himself and his wife, just as Virgil frees Dante at the summit of the Mountain. The whole theme of freedom attained through suffering and enlightenment is, of course, far older than Dante: it is to be found in both the Greek and the Hebraic-Christian roots of our tradition.

That is really my main point: *The Lady from the Sea* may be understood as a picture of Ibsen's tragic theme transcended, and placed in a wider perspective. But before I conclude I wish to qualify this point a bit.

I am not trying to say that Ibsen presents his theme *as* ancient. On the contrary, Ellida's case is ostensibly just incipient insanity, with a few overtones of the occult. If Ibsen was aware of the classic analogies between the purgation of the body and the spirit; between the cleansing of psychiatry, religious conversion, and the purgation accomplished by tragedy, he doesn't suggest it in this play. From the early Renaissance until the middle of the eighteenth century poets and dramatists usually used old stories, the older the better, and they assumed that their audiences wished to recognize, in every play or fable, the ancient commonplaces of moral and religious philosophy: "I tell you what mine authors say" (as

Shakespeare put it). Ibsen's habit was just the opposite. Like his tragic protagonists, he found traditional wisdom all ossified in the dead forms and customs of society and the churches, and he had to reject it completely in order to be himself, and see for himself. He shared this iconoclastic need with most of the live spirits of his time, and appealed to it in his audiences. He presents his plays almost (one might say) for their news value, as though no one before had ever seen what he has just discovered. That is why, if one is to recognize the antiquity of Ibsen's vision as a poet one must dig down below what the characters say, to the movements of their spirits at a level below that of words and concepts. It usually took Ibsen himself about two years to dig down to this level; but there he found not only the amazing theatrical vitality of his plays, but also their perennial significance.

I am not advocating a reading of Ibsen which neglects his sturdy pessimism and his exhilarating icon-smashing. On the contrary, it is those aspects of his work which make him the grandfather of the modern theater; they authenticate his position as a landmark for our time. But in our present "beatnik" world there are no icons left to smash, and if Ibsen speaks to us now it is because the opposite aspect of his work—its timeless poetic insight—can now be seen. In his greatest plays he not only revealed the nineteenth-century *hubris*, the powerful but blind drive of the unsophisticated, the strictly *unregenerate* spirit; he also revealed, with unparalleled courage and candor, what became of that motive. In *The Lady from the Sea*, a sort of footnote to the great tragedies, he saw that catastrophe was not the one predestined end; that the spirit *may* be regenerated. That is why, if we listen closely in reading this play, we may detect echoes of the most venerable themes, and so place Ibsen, where he belongs, among the great explorers of the life of the spirit.

Four Reviews

These reviews were written many years ago, as their dates indicate. They are therefore out of date now: a great deal of work has been done since then, either by the authors I discuss or by others writing about them. I considered trying to revise them, to do justice to those I discuss and to bring out my present opinions. But it soon became evident that that would have been a very big job, requiring more time than I had. I decided, eventually, to use them just as they were written, in the hope that they may throw *some* light on the writers I discuss, at least as they then appeared, and also upon the changes their reputations have undergone in the last twenty years.

James in the Theater

The Complete Plays of Henry James. Edited by Leon Edel.
Lippincott
Partisan Review #6, 1950

"In this volume," Mr. Edel explains, "there appear, collected for the first time, the complete plays of Henry James, together with the unfinished scenario for an unwritten play and sundry prefaces and notes relating to his playwrighting. So far as we know the novelist completed twelve plays in all. Five were published during his lifetime; the remaining seven have never before appeared in public print." In an introductory essay and in forewords to the plays Mr. Edel sketches the theater for which James wrote, in London, and also in America and in France; and he adds enough of James's biography, and enough contemporary criticism of his plays—carefully culled from what must be a vast store of material in letters, newspapers, and memoirs— so that he can follow the whole long story of James's assaults upon the theater almost as though we were there in person. Mr. Edel has done a superb job: he has used the scrupulous methods of scholarship to reveal a pathetic and terrible part of James's story, and also many significant aspects of the modern theater.

It has not been generally realized by critics of James's work that playwrighting was a constant, and very important preoccupation of his for forty years—nor that in his own view and that of a number of experts he came very close to making the grade as a recognized playwright. His first play, *Pyramus and Thisbe,* was written in 1869; as late as 1909 he wrote a monologue for

Ruth Draper. Many managers on both sides of the Atlantic asked him for plays, several were produced; and Mr. Edel shows that his plays commanded at least the interest of many theater-wise people. "So qualified an observer as Bernard Shaw," he writes, "has described the earlier plays as stage-worthy, while rejecting the later works as cast in a dialogue 'inhumanly literary'; while, on the other hand, the equally authoritative Granville-Barker considered the later works, particularly *The Outcry*, to be as manageable as a Restoration play or a play of Chekhov's. . . . Most critics have recognized the high dramatic qualities residing in the plays, as indeed in all the work, of James."

It may be that Shaw and Granville-Barker could judge the theatrical viability of the plays better than we can now. Some of their artificiality and elaborate *politesse* is just old-fashioned. But I must report that I found them—800 double-columned pages of them—unpleasing reading. There are certainly passages of beautifully-built dialogue, wherein the characters make play with the felicitous phrase, delicately distinguishing the finer shades of motive, as in the novels. Once in a while, notably in *Daisy Miller*, a dramatization of the story, one can feel some of James's own themes and sympathies. Sometimes, especially in *The Reprobate*, there is a bit of good farce; and it may be that in farce James could have found a way to make contact between his humanity and that of his audience. But, in general, the plays do not come alive. They are abstract machines without the vital spark; James himself is not in them. His own diagnosis seems to me to be the right one: he "threw the cargo overboard to save the ship." It is too easy to feel the accuracy of a criticism, which Mr. Edel quotes, of a bad production of *The Reprobate* in Boston in 1923: "Blither in a Void." If the dramatist has no respect for his themes and his characters, how can he do anything but blither, and how can the audience do anything but surround the pathetic effort with a void of indifference and incomprehension? James as playwright was at the opposite pole from the miraculous hero of *Once in a Lifetime*. That ex-hoofer had the same reflexes as those of the mythic average man, and therefore he had natural authority on the stage. Whether he wept with sentimentality, dozed, roared with laughter, or ate nuts, his every gesture was immediately clear, he was nature and art at once. But James was painfully conscious of alienation from his audience: he felt invisible and unwanted. He could not charm them with art alone; his efforts to imitate their sentimentalities turned out, too often, to be cold *tours de force*. In reading his plays one feels, very strongly, the failure of his make-believe, the frightening breakdown of communications.

From the point of view of James himself, and his difficult career as an artist, this failure has all the human drama which the plays themselves lack. Mr. Edel has brought this whole story to light. For instance, his narrative of the opening night of *Guy Domville* is a masterpiece of the scholar's art. He shows us James, in flight, attending a performance of Oscar Wilde's *An Ideal Husband*, while the most distinguished audience in London assembled to see his play. In the success of Wilde, James read his own doom; he had a premonition of the hisses which greeted him when he was pushed on stage after the final curtain of *Guy Domville*. We also get a fine picture of the actual performance of that play, as it affected the audience: the well-wishers in the good seats, admiring the fine points, the bored and hostile crowd in the gallery, the breakdown of the actors' authority. The picture one gets of James as stage-struck, as hopelessly wooing a public that wanted none of him, is pathetic and even silly. But Mr. Edel shows, also, that James spared himself none of the flavor of these bewilderments and humiliations.

If James suffered so much from the theater, why did he keep returning to the assault, time and again, for forty years? On the basis of Mr. Edel's evidence, it appears that it is James's long and loving cult of the French Theater, especially the Comédie

Française, which explains both his infatuation with the stage itself, and the sober conviction, which never left him, that he was a born dramatist. It was in Paris that he developed his fine taste in acting. He perceived the wonderful possibilities in the actor's art when there is rigorous training for the actor, standards, an audience of connoisseurs. He thought the Comédie Française a "school of manners," a sign and an agent of the continuing public life of the national spirit, an institution as important in France as Parliament was in England. He could never get out of his mind the notion of such a theater in English, in spite of his accurate sense of the state of the theater in London when he began to write for it, and in spite of his own repeated failures. Mr. Edel gives enough quotations from James's letters and theatrical criticisms to make all this clear. He also refers the reader to *The Scenic Art,* Alan Wade's collection of James's writings on the theater, a very useful companion to Mr. Edel's book.

James's French upbringing in the theater helps to explain his plays and their failure in England. He wanted to write plays for actors who had the conventional and self-conscious art, the glamour, and the snap of the best French acting, and he proceeded to construct well-made "vehicles" like those of Scribe, Dumas, and Augier. The well-made play of the school, developed by Sardou and Scribe, canonized by Sarcey, is a light, firm, all-purpose machine: a concatenation of crystal-clear "situations," in itself nearly empty of human content, but a fine framework for good acting of a certain kind. But James did not find this acting in England, and he never ceased to complain of the amateurishness and stupidity of his actors. If you remove the human vitality and intelligence of actors like Coquelin, the poverty of an intrigue *à la française* is pathetically evident: you get something almost as thin and blithery as James's own plays. When to this artificial plot James adds "the breadsauce of the happy ending," in the hope of hitting the British taste, the effect is sickly indeed.

"Celestial, soothing, sanctifying process" Henry James called his fumbling-out of the dramatic action of his late novels. Upon which Mr. Edel remarks, "The dramatic years—the sacred years—had yielded their full harvest, and not so much in the plays . . . as in the consequences for his fiction arising from their creation." I have believed for many years that the place to study James's drama and its form is the late novels, and not the plays. James himself made a distinction between the "theatrical," which can only live on a particular stage before a particular audience, and the dramatic, which may come alive in the imaginations of scattered readers, each alone under his quiet lamp. In our time the dramas of the late novels have begun to come alive in this way, justifying James's faith in his own gifts as a dramatist, and also confirming the lesson he learned from the theater itself—that to succeed there he had to try to throw his cargo of meaning, of moral content, overboard.

The nature of the drama in *The Golden Bowl*, or *The Ambassdors*, or *The Wings of the Dove*, cannot be understood through a study of James's plays. But one may get a clue to it through studying James's interest in the theater, and especially the French theater. He tried to see through Augier and Dumas to Molière and Racine, by way of the fine actors who performed the whole repertory, very much as he tried to see through the Edwardian drawing-room to the traditional moral, social, human order of which it was the unconscious heir. But I do not elaborate on these points here—I have tried to do so in essays on *The Golden Bowl* and James's conception of dramatic form, the latter to be found on page 48 of this volume.

Though Mr. Edel suggests these problems of interpretation and criticism, he does not explore them in this book. His purpose was to make James's plays, and the actual history of James's struggle with the stage, available at last. He has succeeded admirably, through his very rare combination of scholarship, sympathy, and literary acumen. He is now working on a full-length biography of James. In James's long, lonely life of exploration, the struggle with the theater was only one strand, though an important one. Mr. Edel seems to have both the knowledge and the abilities to give us the whole picture.

On F. R. Leavis

The Common Pursuit. By F. R. Leavis. George W. Stewart
Partisan Review #2, 1953

"The common pursuit of true judgement" is a phrase in
Eliot's "The Function of Criticism" which Mr. Leavis uses to
define his own aim and method: "That," he writes, "is how the
critic should see his business, and what it should be for him. His
perceptions and judgments are his, or they are nothing; but,
whether or not he has consciously addressed himself to co-opera-
tive labor, they are inevitably collaborative. Collaboration may
take the form of disagreement, and one is grateful to the critic
whom one has found worth disagreeing with." Thus Mr. Leavis
assumes a common interest in literature on the part of his
readers and the other critics he mentions; they are all to compare notes, and defend their impressions and opinions with a
certain decent pugnacity. At the same time he feels that the
whole attempt to cultivate the art of letters is threatened in
our time, and in its defense he is ready to take on all comers.
From time to time he will pause in the discussion of literature
long enough to slay a pedant or a middle-brow book-section editor with great gusto and elegance.

Mr. Leavis pursues the true judgment of many English
writers, including Milton, Hopkins, Swift, Pope, Johnson, Bunyan,
Shakespeare, James, Forster, Lawrence, and Eliot. His starting
point is usually some judgment which he disagrees with; he
seems to depend on disagreement for his stimulus and his occa-

sion. He then makes his own point in a fine, civilized, essayistic and conversational style, based on taste and the perception of literary values. The result is a book to which one can hardly do justice in a review. It should be read slowly, at intervals, and mulled over; used in that way it could hardly fail to sharpen one's enjoyment and promote the development of accurate insight. Is anything more to be asked of a book of literary criticism? I think not; Mr. Leavis is the very model of the accomplished literary critic in English, and if one feels some dissatisfaction and loss of confidence in reading his book, it is probably dissatisfaction with the "modern criticism" which Mr. Leavis has done so much to perfect, rather than with his performance in that art.

"The formula for Johnson as critic," Mr. Leavis writes, "is this: he is strong where an Augustan training is in place, and his limitations appear when the training begins to manifest itself as unjustifiable resistance. That 'unjustified,' of course, will involve an appeal to one's own judgement. I myself judge that Johnson discriminates with something approaching infallibility between what is strong and what is weak in the eighteenth century." This is an illuminating observation on Johnson, and it suggests a close analogy between him and Mr. Leavis. Mr. Leavis' training seems to us to be wider and deeper than Johnson's, enabling him to appreciate Johnson's limitations as well as his virtues. The fact that he does have a training gives him strength and sureness of touch, but in his work also I feel from time to time an "unjustified resistance" which seems to show limitations in the training (and the art) of his "modern criticism."

Take, for example, two of Mr. Leavis' treatments of Shakespeare. He has four essays largely devoted to Shakespeare, all good; but in all of them he stops at the very point where I should like to see him continue, as though something in his conception of criticism, or even in his style, resisted further investigation. His starting point in "Tragedy and the 'Medium'" is Santayana's comparison between Macbeth's "Tomorrow and tomorrow" and Piccarda de Donati's celebrated *"E'n la sua voluntade è nostra pace,"* from the *Paradiso.* Santayana had written, "In Shakespeare the medium is rich and thick and more important than the idea; whereas in Dante the medium is as unvarying and simple as possible, and meant to be transparent. . . . A clear and transparent medium is admirable when we love what we have to say; but when what we have to say is nothing previously definite, expressiveness depends on stirring the waters deeply suggesting a thousand half-thoughts. . . . The medium then becomes dominant: but can this be called success in expression? It is rather success in making an impression, if the reader is impressed." To which Mr. Leavis retorts, "The critic who falls so complete a victim to the word 'medium' as Mr. Santayana here shows himself, doesn't, it is plain, understand the poetic—and the essentially dramatic—use of language that Shakespeare's verse supremely exemplifies. He cannot, then, understand the nature of the organization that goes with that use of language: he cannot appreciate the ways in which the themes and significances of the play are dramatically presented." I think Mr. Leavis is right, and Santayana wrong. Mr. Leavis must be seeing *Macbeth* more adequately and judging it more truly; but what then *is* the organization of the play which Santayana missed, and what are some of the essentially dramatic ways whereby Shakespeare conveys the meaning he intends? Mr. Leavis does not tell us. He goes on to more general questions about tragedy, but he throws no further light on *Macbeth:* he rests his case on the validity of his over-all judgment.

In *Measure for Measure* also he judges that that play is consistent in form, and among the most significant and ethically sensitive of Shakespeare's works; and in this I agree too. Yet Mr. Leavis says little to substantiate that view beyond observations on some of the characters. He refers to G. Wilson Knight's essay with approval, but does not explore his Christian inter-

pretation any further, as Professor Battenhouse did so ably in his
Measure for Measure and Christian Doctrine of the Atonement,
illuminating thereby many complex passages and dramatic situations. Here too one feels that there is something in Mr. Leavis'
conception of literary criticism, perhaps his emphasis on "judgement" as its aim, perhaps too exclusive a reliance on "sensibility," which makes him stop short of conclusive and completely
lucid analysis. He prefers to safeguard the fertile mystery of
literature: a laudable policy, but one which after twenty years
of modern criticism seems to show diminishing returns.

In "Henry James and the Function of Criticism" Mr. Leavis
discusses Mr. Quentin Anderson's essay on James's last three
novels, in which Mr. Anderson demonstrated an elaborate
Swedenborgian allegory culminating in *The Golden Bowl.* Mr.
Leavis gives full credit to Mr. Anderson for his discovery of the
allegory, which he accepts, but adds, "My main criticism of Mr.
Anderson is that he is not, in his interpretation of James, actively
enough a literary critic: his use of the key seems to be something
apart from his critical sensibility." That is probably right, and
Mr. Anderson himself, in his essay, had pointed out that further
work was to be done in relating the allegorical acheme to the
actual language and drama of the novel. But Mr. Leavis does
not proceed to attempt that task. Instead he gives us his judgment that late James is morally distasteful and comparatively
empty of life. I do not have much confidence in that judgment.
It seems to rest on other resistances in Mr. Leavis, notably a
resistance to James's picture of the rich Middle Western Ververs
in *The Golden Bowl.* Mr. Leavis wants to regard the American
rich as vulgar, hearty pirates or guileless optimists. I admit
that I have had little chance to observe them in their fabulous,
inaccessible world, but I do not think that innocence of any sort
will go far toward accounting for them. I can believe in the terrible struggle for power which James shows the Ververs winning
against Charlotte and the Prince—by dint of the power of their

money, it is true, but also by gloomy tenacity of will. The Ververs are just about as innocent as Eliot's Thomas á Becket, whose final temptation is to use his spiritual power for worldly ends and "rule from the tomb." They are akin to the alienated, discarnate Adamses, a type of American "idealist" that seems destined to play a crucial part in the contemporary world struggle for power. The crucial question about them is not whether they are innocent, but whether they are evil. Mr. Leavis does not sense either the toughness or the prescience in *The Golden Bowl*.

Both James and Eliot learned early in their careers to address the English, if not in their language, at least in the language they *ought* to have had. Both had their English literary careers after absorbing some very un-English impressions. In Eliot's case these included modern French poetry, Dante, Harvard Buddhism, Mark Twain's Mississippi, and I do not know what other outlandish elements. And both of them, late in their careers, entered a phase in which their literary attainments in England came to have for them only a secondary, symbolic value. I think it is significant that Mr. Leavis likes them both best as English men of letters, and has little light to shed either on their genesis or on their final explorations. It was from the early Eliot that Mr. Leavis got his first clues to literary criticism. In this book he is still practicing that art, and in several places, notably the first essay, "Mr. Eliot and Milton," he feels obliged to defend it from Mr. Eliot himself as he is now, with his political and religious preoccupations, his comparatively tepid enthusiasm for literature as such.

We must be very grateful that Mr. Leavis is all in literature, for in that lies the inestimable value of his work. I hope that modern criticism will not stay in its present phase; Mr. Leavis' virtuosity shows that it has reached a point of mastery after which some new development is needed. But Mr. Leavis' trained sensibility is something which is and will continue to be badly needed, and every part of his book shows it. Consider the way he pays his respects to the Cambridge intellectuals who patronized D. H. Lawrence: "Articulateness and unreality cultivated together; callowness disguised from itself in articulateness; conceit casing itself safely in a confirmed sense of high sophistication; the uncertainty as to whether one is serious or not taking itself for ironic poise; who has not at some time observed the process?" Who indeed?—though usually in academic circles without much of the Cambridge brilliance. Mr. Leavis' attack, in defense of literary sensibility, is itself literature, accurate and final and heartening as only excellent writing can be.

Auden in Mid-Career

Auden. By Richard Hoggart. Yale University Press
Partisan Review #4, 1952

Mr. Hoggart says: "This essay is meant to be an introduction only, a running of the finger down certain aspects of Auden's verse, so that the general reader may turn to it more readily." Mr. Hoggart succeeded with me: his book led me to re-read Auden himself. But having done so, I find that I am somewhat dissatisfied with what Mr. Hoggart has done. I wish that he had gone a little bit farther, ventured upon a few generalizations—in short, been more explicit about his picture of Auden's art and its development. There is much to be said for trying to introduce a poet to new readers, instead of judging him; yet some sort of bias is inevitable, and perhaps it is better to admit it clearly. Mr. Hoggart's book may be described as a reading of Auden, with many quotations, and with elucidations of passages and stylistic devices; and it is apparently addressed to readers who do not yet like modern verse.

In commending Auden to his general reader, Mr. Hoggart lays great emphasis on Auden's insight into the notorious Plight of Our Time. He quotes Auden: "In grasping the character of a society, as in judging the character of an individual, no documents, statistics, 'objective' measurements can ever compete with the single intuitive glance." And he applies the formula to Auden's verse: "It is this kind of perception which allows Auden to pass his eye over a situation, a web of relationships or a complex of emotional nuances, and detect the typical feature, the important connection. . . . Its lucidity is both exciting and liberating to the reader, presumably because it sets some part of what was previously amorphous into a high selective but revealing pattern:

> And nervous people who will never marry
> Live upon dividends in the old world cottages
> With an animal for friend and a volume of memoirs."

This is a fair sample of Mr. Hoggart's rather awkward writing, and it indicates his own interest in Auden as a seer. When he says that Auden's lucidity is exciting and liberating, he is right; but if the reader seeks in Auden for some consistent diagnosis of our social life—what we look for (without necessarily finding) in philosophy or history—he will be disappointed. Auden's lucidity is not that of thought, but of ceaseless thoughtfulness; not that of stable knowledge, but of the apt phrase; in short, it is a striking quality of his poetic *medium*. Eliot says that the poet has not a personality to express, but a medium. I don't think Eliot meant that the poet's medium was the poet's language, but the distinction is hard to make, especially in Auden's case. In him, perception and epithet, attitude and meaning, tone and content are one.

Mr. Hoggart devotes his first three chapters to a description of Auden's writing in general, with the purpose of making things easier for the new reader. There are many details which one would like to argue about in these chapters; but a pretty just impression of Auden's poetic medium somehow emerges from them. We are reminded of the conceptual basis of his language; its resources of caricature and parody; its sometimes rather hysterical snobbishness, which Mr. Hoggart deplores; its extraordinary flexibility. Auden's voice is always very recognizably his own, yet at the same time he can catch the tones of more other writers than anyone else except Joyce. Mr. Hoggart points out passages which sound like the Sagas, Browning, Blake, Skelton, Yeats, Eliot, and others—besides popular verse of various times and places. There is a mimetic element at the root of his poetic gift, but it is verbal and musical, and neither visual nor dramatic, as Mr. Hoggart rightly observes. My own impression is that Auden's musical talent is even more fundamental to his art than his witty conceptualizing. His best poems are carried by the song, and by his wonderful dexterity with the arabesques of many different verse-forms.

Auden is perhaps the most obviously gifted poet we have, with an inborn fluency in verse comparable to Shaw's in theatrical conversation, or Aldous Huxley's is sardonic narrative. These authors are conscious of being able to say a great deal very well; the voluble demon presses them day and night. The question which bothers them is *what* to say—not whether. The last four chapters of Mr. Hoggart's book are on Auden's themes. He shows that Auden has been talking about love (like so many poets before him) throughout his career. But his early themes, before he came to America, are largely Freudian and Marxian, while since then they have been Christian by way of Kierkegaard, Niebuhr, Charles Williams, and Eliot. Mr. Hoggart approaches Auden's themes with his usual modesty, and he is again helpful in his elucidations and quotations. But because of his interest in Auden's prophetic role, he takes the themes, if not too seriously, at least seriously in a misleading way. There is no doubt, for instance, that Auden, like everyone else, has absorbed countless homeopathic doses of Freudianism; his system was soaked in it at an early age. But there is not much evidence that he ever tried to think out its relation to other views of the psyche's life, or to ask himself in cold blood whether he was living by that philosophy. Freudianism appears in the verse of his Freudian period like the semi-ironic echoes of other poets —with light quotation marks, and with a witty and briefly illuminating effect. As for his Marxism, that comes through chiefly as enthusiasm and sloganizing, all half-disowned by the prevailing tone of parody.

Auden's Christian themes are more difficult to assess, because we don't know the relation between "new styles of architecture" and "a change of heart." Auden has announced the change of heart, and Mr. Hoggart very properly assumes it, making the important point that "there has not been a sudden reversal of outlook, but rather a continuous development in a mind of great honesty and sublety applying itself fruitfully to its own field of experience." And certainly this change, or development, is reflected in the gradual change in his themes. His style, on the other hand, has come through apt and fluent as ever, reflecting Christian writers as it once did Freud or Groddeck, and snobbishly classifying the sons of God with the old omniscient nonchalance:

> Blessed Woman,
> Excellent Man,
> Redeem for the dull the
> Average Way,
> That Common ungifted
> Natures may
> Believe that their normal
> Vision can
> Walk to perfection.

So he murmurs to Saint Joseph and the Virgin Mary in his *Christmas Oratorio*, leaning out of heaven with them, sure that they will understand his tender concern for the common ungifted natures below. There is no doubt that the intention is Christian; but what is the effect? Somewhat uncommited, I think; too close to the ironic invocation in *The Dance of Death:*

> Vital young man
> Do what you can
> For our dust
> We who are weak
> Want a splendid physique.

But I do not know as much as Auden himself does about the difficulty of adapting his style, a habit of many years' growth, to his new belief:

> Can I learn to suffer
> Without saying something ironic or funny
> On suffering?

Prospero (who stands for Shakespeare who stands for Auden) asks this question in the course of the seven pages of verse in which he explains to Ariel that he is giving up verse in favor of the pursuit of sanctity. It is a Christian version of the Plight of the Artist, on which Auden has had more to say than anyone else except Thomas Mann. If I were going to investigage Auden's present Christianity, I should study what he says now about the artist, the field of experience nearest home. Mr. Hoggart has pointed out several good places to do that, notably Caliban's terribly difficult speech in *The Sea and the Mirror*.

Mr. Hoggart does not think that the longer pieces, the plays, *New Year Letter*, *The Sea and the Mirror*, *The Age of Anxiety*, and *For the Time Being*, are quite successful as wholes, though he points out beautiful passages in each. I think he is right, but I wish he had speculated about the reason. Auden is not alone in wishing to proceed from the short lyric to some more capacious form, and being somewhat thrwarted in the attempt. It would be interesting to compare his experience in this respect with Eliot's or Wallace Stevens'.

Mr. Hoggart thinks that the songs, and in general many short poems, are Auden's most unqualified successes. I agree with him again, and wish again that he had tried to investigate the magic of the songs, one or two of the early *Odes*, and *Paid on Both Sides*, a work which Mr. Hoggart (following Auden, who has not wished to reprint it) unjustly neglects. To my taste it is the most original, and the best, longer work. The scene, a country ruined by industry now rotting in its turn; the mythology, oddly suggestive of the Sagas, prep-school athletics, Sophocles, spy-stories; and the language, which is mannered but wonderfully musical, all compose. It is the only longer work which is not devised: the idea itself is just that long and complex, an authentic nightmare.

My chief quarrel with the impression of Auden that Mr. Hoggart gives is that he has not stressed sufficiently that talent for music, the music of language, which produces something beautiful whenever Auden is not too bothered by intellectual problems. The ultimate question about Mr. Hoggart's book is whether his general reader exists—whether it is possible to interest someone who does not already like poetry, in Auden. But for readers who are interested in modern poetry, the book is useful; and its modest, descriptive method is appropriate for a study of Auden, who is not to be placed or judged at this moment: he is in mid-career, and more acutely conscious of the problems of his art than his critics can be.

Sartre as Playwright

Partisan Review #4, 1949

Perhaps it is not too soon to offer observations on Sartre's dramaturgy, and on his sudden career in the American Theater. I take as my text three of his plays: *No Exit,* as produced by the *Theatre Intime* in Princeton, *The Victors,* produced by New Stages in their Bleecker Street theater, and *Red Gloves,* the Jed Harris production, late of the Mansfield.

No Exit was the first of Sartre's plays to attract wide attention in this country. Garcin, a pacifist who subtly betrayed his cause, his comrades and his wife; Inez, a lesbian who drove a man and a woman to their deaths, and Estelle, a faithless wife who drove her lover to suicide, have died and meet in Hell. Hell consists for them in the fact that they are confined together in an ugly second empire parlor. They are literally everything to each other, for they can see themselves, confirm their own existences, only in each other's eyes. They begin to hate each other after the first five minutes; for they discover that they can get no satisfaction from each other, not even that of lust. Estelle is not a lesbian, and she and Garcin cannot get together because Garcin suffers from a kind of guilty *pudeur,* he loses his enthusiasm when Inez, watching his advances to the willing Estelle, makes scornful comments. Garcin puts his plight succinctly: "Hell is other people." When this little trap has been explained with great dialectical ingenuity and with mounting

143

suspense, the three see that their punishment is to consist of an eternity of each other's murderous scrutiny; and the curtain falls.

The Victors was adapted by Thornton Wilder from Sartre's *Morts Sans Sépulture*. I think Mr. Wilder did a competent and faithful job of translation, but I am judging on the basis of the performance which seemed to me to preserve the intent of the original. The acting (which was in general good, and sometimes superb) may account for a good deal of the vitality of the play. The story is that of a group of Maquis captured by the Vichy police, at about the time of the early Allied victories in Normandy. The police torture the captives, to make them reveal the whereabouts of their leader. The Maquis are a varied group, illustrating every possible attitude to torture, from an experienced revolutionary who takes it calmly, to a fifteen-year-old boy who collapses at the mere thought, and including one woman. The leader himself is added to this group when the police arrest him, not knowing who he is; and though he is in no physical danger, he is soon morally "engaged" in the ordeal, and suffers a more painful case of *Angst* than the actual victims. Upon this situation Sartre plays many ingenious variations. One of the men murders the boy, and then engages in some painful casuistry to justify the murder. The woman is raped, and the physical coward commits suicide. In the final scene, when the leader has been released, the captives can reveal his former hiding place without betraying the cause; and this produces a new *cas de conscience* for them to debate: is it better to go free, or to stay, for the sake of thwarting their tormentors? They finally decide for freedom, but one of the policemen shoots them anyway to indulge in purely personal appetite for cruelty.

Jed Harris's production of *Red Gloves*, adapted by Daniel Taradash from *Les Mains Sales*, was a skillful job of denaturing Sarte for the Broadway market. *Les Mains Sales*, as Sartre wrote it, is a grim contemporary parable of *Existenz*, illustrating the same metaphysical extremity as all his other plays. Hugo, a young man from a well-to-do family in a central European country, has joined the Communist Party because he feels the need to prove himself in action, and has an idealistic faith (which Sartre does not share) in the redemptive destiny of the proletariat. The Russians are beginning to drive the German armies back; soon they will arrive. Hoederer (the local Communist chief) wants to make a coalition with the liberals and conservatives in order to take power as bloodlessly as possible, but the comrades think this a betrayal of the Party line, and they decree that Hoederer must be liquidated. Hugo volunteers for this job, is made Hoederer's secretary, and, with his nice young wife Jessica, moves into the old palace where the Party has its headquarters. But when he actually sees Hoederer, and hears his side of the story, he doesn't want to kill him. Thus he is caught in an impossible situation: he does not recognize his moral freedom either in murdering or not murdering; it is the familiar existential mixture of pride and self-hatred, intensified by an obsessive need to make a crucial decision. His wife unwittingly helps him out of this blind alley: bored with his indecision, she makes love to Hoederer. Hoederer demurs at first; an affair with Jessica would ruin a good secretary; but at last (candidly explaining that he hasn't had a woman in six months) he sighs and kisses her. This little vacation from Party matters is his undoing: Hugo catches them and shoots Hoederer. This, however, solves nothing for Hugo. He is sent to prison for the murder, but released with the other political prisoners when the Russians arrive, and he carries his existential problem right along with him. Was the murder heroism—the gesture of a big man of action such as he had always wanted to be—or was it a more bourgeois crime of passion? He also finds, when he is released, and looks up his tough Party mistress, Olga, that the Party line has changed: Hoederer's policy of boring from within has been adopted, and Hoederer is canonized as a martyr to the orthodox cause. Hugo's crucial choice now appears in other terms, closer to what Sartre thinks of as the one reality of the human situation: He may either rejoin the party in another country under another name, or keep his name, together with the blame or credit for the murder. Since the murder is all he has to call his own, the only sign of his existence, he chooses the latter alternative, and cheerfully marches off with the comrades to be liquidated.

Mr. Taradash's *Red Gloves* keeps the main facts of this typical and very skillful Sartre plot. His changes were chiefly cuts, in the role of Olga, Hugo's communist mistress (reduced in his version to a perfunctory lay figure who merely gives information) and in the scenes between Hugo and Jessica. But the effect of these cuts was to make a very different play, in which Hugo is no longer the protagonist, and the existential theme is almost lost to sight. In *Les Mains Sales* we learn (mostly by way of Hugo's relation to Olga) that he identifies himself with Raskolnikov, and even took the name of this hero to use in the Party. Thus he inherits the sterile willfulness of that long line of lost young highbrows who are Sartre's own ancestors—Julien Sorel, Ivan Karamazov, Gide's immoralist, and the rest; and so we understand more richly the absurd incommensurability between his platonic infatuation with the idea of action, and the Realpolitik of the comrades themselves. In *Les Mains Sales* the relation between Hugo and Jessica is also much more developed than it is in *Red Gloves;* and Sartre completely understands their childish eroticism, so abstract and irresponsible that it is hardly sexual at all. In the economy of his play, this relationship establishes the background of futility, emptiness, and moral anarchy which we must have if we are to accept Hugo's compulsion to murder. When Mr. Taradash drastically reduced these elements, he cut most of the crazy intensity out of the role of Hugo, leaving Hoederer the center of interest. In the performance, Boyer's authority and intelligence also helped to make that role overshadow all the rest, and to turn the play into a study of a saintly commissar (Yogi and thug in one) who is martyrized by his myopic associates.

I have remarked that Messrs. Harris and Taradash between them did a skillful job of transforming Sartre's sardonic parable into the sleek suburban terms of serious, or "better," Broadway. The production was handsome, and granted that version of the play, the acting was good. John Dall, for instance, as Hugo, was certainly not acting the role which Sartre wrote, but he offered a shrewd and humorous portrait of a mildly leftish young American with horn-rimmed spectacles, a B.A. in Social Studies, and a minor job in the New Deal. One could not believe that such a young man would be that kind of a martyr to a theory of himself; the American analogue of Hugo would be Leopold or Loeb, rather than our bachelors of arts who take up government work and get into messes with Communism. In the same way, Joan Tetzel was charming as a nice young wife who is bored with her husband; but she was far from presenting the amoral little kitten Sartre had in mind.

These three plays, though the productions they received were different, and also the audiences they met, all proved to have great theatrical viability. There is no doubt that Sartre has found a way to make himself heard, even in our jaded and confused theaters. He has the authentic playwright's gift for living speech, and for characters with the immediate impact of newsreel closeups. He is also an extremely resourceful plotmaker in the French tradition—the French word for plot is "intrigue." It would be a mistake to dismiss his plays merely because his existentialism is so feeble as ethics or epistemology. But his philosophy did lead him to his dramaturgic formula. He writes a "drama of crisis" on the analogy of Barth's "theology of crisis"; and it is this existentialist slant that gives the new look to his moral casuistry and his gripping well-made plots.

Each of his plays illustrates the extreme, or existential situation, but his style has changed and grown a good deal. In his

first plays he tries to put his metaphysical point unrealistically:
in *The Flies* by means of the Orestes myth, in *No Exit* by the
metaphor of Hell. But his didacticism is too violent and literal for
this style (which he may have learned from Giraudoux) and
the photographic realism of *The Respectful Prostitute, The Victors,* and *Red Gloves* serves his purposes better. Contemporary
life offers plenty of extreme situations, with all the authority of
the headline and all the fascination of the street-accident. He
found one in this country also—that of the Negro unjustly accused of murder. I can think of another which he has over-
looked: a visit to the dentist. Here too we have an inescapable
ordeal with an obsessive power; a form of torment which threatens the very basis of human freedom, and which only the heroic
can survive with dignity:

> Beneath the bludgeoning of fate
> My head is bloody but unbowed.

And this situation is more austerely existential than most of the
ones he has used: it is more abstract, and may the more easily
by considered apart from ultimate values.

I think that all three audiences which I observed at his
plays, though unquestionably held during the performance,
were in the long run somewhat let down by this abstract nature
of his basic situation—the moral crisis considered apart from ultimate common values. "I have suppressed God the Father," he
tells us; and he adds that there is no such thing as human nature. He is consistent enough to suppress also all the up-to-date
versions of a common end: he is not interested in the Communism of his characters in *Red Gloves,* nor in the Cause of his
Maquis in *The Victors,* nor in the actual problem of racial justice
in the South—these issues merely precipitate extreme situations
which illustrate his peculiar moral athleticism in a meaningless
world. The *Red Gloves* production softened this metaphysical

anarchism, inviting the rather puzzled audience to interpret the play in a long-suffering liberal sense. The productions of *No Exit* and of *The Victors,* by the Princeton undergraduates and New Stages respectively, were true to the plays he wrote, and both had the honesty and disinterested pleasure in the theater which which Broadway seldom offers; I am sorry I lack the space to do justice to these performances. But there too the audiences seemed slightly puzzled and unsatisfied, and for the same reason. The highbrow, socially-conscious Bleecker Street audience would seem to be the right one for Sartre, if we have it at all; but I thought they were first piqued, and then disappointed, to discover that *The Victors* was not an anti-Vichy tract.

The American theater, trying to be up-to-date, groping about for material with some life in it, has received Sartre with enthusiasm and treated him as handsomely as it could, both on and off Broadway. But on the whole this encounter does not look very auspicious. As for Sartre himself, probably it would be necessary to see him in the livelier theatrical life of Paris, where he is only one voice in an animated but not too serious discussion which has been going on for a long time, in order to place him in the proper perspective. Our dispersed, spasmodic, and undernourished theater has nothing to digest him with. Until and unless we develop some sort of continuous theatrical life of our own, we shall be in the position of eavesdropping upon a conversation in the next flat, trying to make sense out of the fragments we get, and usually mistaking the most emphatic remarks for the most pregnant.

ABOUT THE AUTHOR

Francis Fergusson was born in Albuquerque, New Mexico; he studied at Harvard College and, as a Rhodes Scholar, at Queen's College, Oxford. After several years as associate director of the American Laboratory Theatre, he became dramatic critic for *The Bookman* magazine. He began his teaching career at the New School for Social Research; from 1934 to 1947 he taught at Bennington College, and was also director of its College Theatre. Professor Fergusson worked at Princeton's Institute for Advanced Study in 1948 and 1949, and was Director of the Princeton Seminars in Literary Criticism from 1949 to 1952. He spent 1952-53 as visiting professor of literature at Indiana University. In 1953 he was appointed University Professor of Comparative Literature at Rutgers University; he retired in 1968 to devote his time to further research and writing.

Mr. Fergusson's books include *The Idea of a Theatre* (1949); *Dante's Drama of the Mind* (1953), which received the Christian Gauss Award of the Phi Beta Kappa Society in 1954; *The Human Image in Dramatic Literature* (1957); *Dante* (1966); and *Shakespeare: The Pattern in His Carpet* (1970). He has written critical introductions to the plays of Molière (1950), to Aristotle's *Poetics* (1961), and to sixteen of Shakespeare's plays. His poems have been published extensively in *Poetry* magazine and in such quarterlies as *Partisan Review* and *Sewanee Review;* in 1962 Rutgers University Press published *Poems,* a collection of his verse. He is also extremely well known as a lecturer and book reviewer; he has been general editor of the Laurel Shakespeare Editions since 1957. In addition to the Christian Gauss Award, he was given the Annual Award for Literature of the National Institute of Arts and Letters in 1953, and has received two honorary doctorates, from the University of New Mexico in 1955 and from Rutgers University in 1975.